Tuning In Your Family Vision and Living It Out

Sayer Strauch

WHAT'S MY FAMILY'S STORY?

We want to hear from you. Please send your comments about this book to us in care of the address noted below.

comments@highdefinitionfamily.com
or visit:
www.highdefinitionfamily.com

Copyright © 2009 by Sayer Strauch

The High Definition Family
by Sayer Strauch

Printed in the United States of America

ISBN 9781615791354

All rights reserved solely by the author. The author guarantees all contents are original and do not infringe upon the legal rights of any other person or work. No part of this publication may be reproduced, stored in a retrieval system, or transmitted in any form or by any means—electronic, mechanical, photocopy, recording, or any other—except for brief quotations in printed reviews, without the prior permission of the author. Requests for information or permissions must be made in writing to the above address. The views expressed in this book are not necessarily those of the publisher.

Unless otherwise indicated, Bible quotations are taken from the following:

AMP	Amplified Version Grand Rapids: Zondervan (1965)
CEV	Contemporary English Version New York: American Bible Society (1995)
KJV	King James Version (1611)
LB	Living Bible Wheaton, IL: Tyndale House Publishers (1979)
MSG	The Message Colorado Springs: Navpress (1993)
NCV	New Century Version Dallas: Word Bibles (1991)
NIRV	New International Revised Version International Bible Society and Zondervan (1996)
NIV	New International Version Colorado Springs: International Bible Society (1978, 1984)
NLT	New Living Translation Wheaton, IL: Tyndale House Publishers (1996)
NRSV	New Revised Standard Version Grand Rapids: Zondervan (1990)

Illustrations by Sayer Strauch, Copyright © 2009 Sayer Strauch

www.xulonpress.com

Contents

Vision

The High Definition Family

A High Definition Journey
Your Family's Own Journey

The viewing and listening experience of High Definition televisions seems worlds apart from that of older sets. HDTVs provide a more vivid and dynamic combination of sharper visual clarity and enhanced sound. You see blades of grass where before you saw only a field. You see movement as dynamically three-dimensional where before you saw a slow and distant two-dimensional blur. This book provides guidance for a high definition journey that will dynamically transform the structure, assumptions and paradigm—the definition—you live with as a family.

Our vision for creating this book for you is to participate with God in coaching, guiding and inspiring you to reach your fullest potential in alignment with God, moving us all forward in a movement only God can lead.

The High Definition Family will guide you and your family in applying five core biblical principles:

- **Choice**
- **Self-Awareness**
- **Awareness of God**
- **Vision**
- **The High Definition Family**

Be ready for God's guidance, encouragement, and inspiration as you embark on this journey. These five principles guide you in taking hold of the opportunities that God will provide for weaving your own story into the unfolding story of God for the world. What if you and your family were to begin your own high definition journey with God, right now? *Let's get started!*

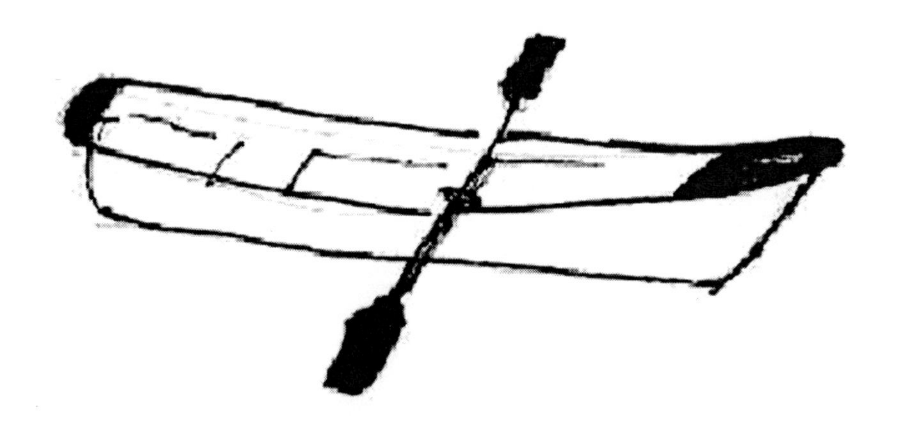

Principle #1: Choice

My choice is you, God, first and only. And now I find I'm your choice! You set me up with a house and yard. And then you made me your heir!

— **Psalm 16:5** (MSG)

Seeing Your Family's Journey as a Story

"Leave your country…and go to the land I will show you. I will make you into a great nation and I will bless you. I will make your name great, and you will be a blessing."

Genesis 12:1-12 (NIV)

"What's Our Story?"

We married late, in our mid-30's. We lived in a beautiful little northwest town, Clatskanie, Oregon. Our brick house had a modest lawn and beautiful rose bushes in front, a spot for a vegetable garden, and two big fruitful blueberry bushes in the back corner.

While still often engaged in what our friends were calling our "put-love-notes-on-the-bathroom-mirror phase," we were settling in with the challenging task of joining our lives together. We had our first fight—can't remember what about. Heidi has an emotional intensity that I wasn't accustomed to. With my heart pounding with fight-or-flight adrenaline and confusion, I was scared. I flew! Some guys go to the local bar—I flew to the side yard! I went out to the two humongous blueberry bushes big enough to hide in to find some serenity to deal with what I didn't know how to deal with.

I had an excuse—a large plastic bowl for picking berry after juicy berry. After ten minutes I heard the side screen door creak open. Heidi walked over. She knew this was my sanctuary for reflection. She quietly smiled and joined me in picking berries and a calm began to fall on both of us.

Our story was just beginning. If there were a book called ***Conflict for Dummies*** I would have been the dummy the book was intended for. We've now been married nine years. I had learned from my own family upbringing and experiences to shy away from conflict, to fly away like a bird landing on a barbecue grill fired-up to blazing. Yet early in our sixth year *(yes, it took that long)*, I made a conscious shift in finding the gumption to stand firm and switch from flight to fight, to represent my concerns and feelings as vigorously as Heidi.

Recently, however, I realized that I still didn't have it right. I was being more bold but not necessarily more loving toward Heidi. I began to ask God for wisdom in how I could wisely and lovingly respond in the midst of conflict. Shortly after, I was reminded to use and apply a practice of centering prayer, letting go, profoundly experiencing and aligning with God both during the prayer time and in moments of stress or conflict.

The results were staggering. Suddenly, I seemed to be making deposits in Heidi's emotional bank account. I felt more loving and accepting toward her. I no longer felt threatened by her intense emotion and now felt as though I could lovingly engage with her no matter what emotions she might intensely express.

I (Heidi) grew up in a family with six children, a mom, a dad, and a step-mom. Most of us have an emotional intensity that can be intimidating. I married an exceptional man who grew up in a family that was more reserved. I have to deal with conflict now so I don't implode. I know that the only way to the other side of conflict is through: there is no around, over, under, or camping out on the near side. But how to walk through in a way that grows our relationship rather than stunts it? How do I express myself in a way that shows love and respect?

During our first year or so of marriage, when Sayer and I experienced conflict I found it difficult to express myself without being hurtful. But we invested a lot of time and energy in working through even the smallest conflicts, knowing that those can become devastating through the years as our story unfolds. Many times, Sayer needed space and walked out back to the blueberry bush with a bowl for picking. I would wait awhile, until I knew that I was ready to truly listen, then would grab a bowl and go out. We would pick berries silently together, sometimes for a long time, before we were both ready to listen and to speak.

Along with occasionally using marriage counseling, I think the most effective thing we did was to pray, alone and together, for the courage to look at ourselves and our own behavior and to own up to it, knowing that this makes us vulnerable. We both knew that it wasn't about winning an argument, but about learning how to love each other better, to be an anchor for each other to go out into the world and love others.

Whether you are a single mother or father, a couple engaged to be married, a couple with young children or an older couple, you are unique and uniquely on a journey with highs and lows as you go day-to-day. Yet, by choosing to see your family journey as a story, you recognize that the choices you make in life critically shape who you are and are becoming. These choices shape your character, behavior, relationships, and your influence upon others.

You have this book in hand for your family and for such a time as this. God wants you and your family to become all it is created on Earth to do and be. Yet, this is not about becoming "the ideal family," a perfect family, or even a good family, but about *your* family as you are now, on an adventure with God reaching your highest potential. If you don't know what makes your family unique then you have no defined context for making decisions and you become defined by the history of your own messy family and the messy world you live in. *And that can be, well, messy.*

Many of us have a love-hate relationship with our family experience. On the one hand, we go through phases of joy, laughter, and playfulness in knowing we are part of a family. On the other hand, we experience pain and sadness in how our family life seems isolated from what God is doing for the world. Many feel too overwhelmed with the messiness of their own family story to begin to engage with God's story for the world. Yet, ultimately, most of us long to be part of something bigger than ourselves.

And God is up to something bigger than ourselves. What is God's story? God is on the move for people. God isn't so much interested in religion—that is, humankind's efforts to reach God (imagine Jesus' harsh interaction with many of the "religious" experts or Pharisees).[1] God is interested in relationships. God is interested in people hanging their hat with God. God wants folks to explore and then commit to a relationship with God, relying upon God and not their own efforts. And God wants these folks as partners to donate this unconditional love to others and to nurture others' acceptance of God's free gift of this love. God wants these folks to join in the unfolding story of God.

God interrupted human history when God called upon Abraham, saying he would have descendants as numerous as the stars in the sky. God called out through Abraham a new nation, the Israelites, to be a blessing to the world, to prepare the way for the coming of God's Son. God interrupted human history with Jesus' birth among the Israelites. Jesus' ministry and journey to the cross realize a whole new realm: God's on the planet. God is getting this new reality out into the corners of the world and the depths of every soul.

God has a heart for you and for everyone. As Bill Hybels so well said, every person you lock eyes with is someone God passionately wants to be reconnected with.[2] God is constantly on the move in nurturing every person to respond to God's call to be reunited. This is God's unfolding story, a high definition story for the world.

Yet the messiness of our own family history clouds not only our relationships with each other but with God. Without a vision, we might occasionally become inspired to expand beyond our own private world but our family life itself has no vision that consistently orients us as a family, let alone beyond ourselves. The Bible has it right that where there is no vision, the people—in this case the family—perish.[3] Oh, the family may still exist but its messy story becomes hopelessly messier and not intentionally part of what God is doing for the world.

Your Vision is Your Story

But there is good news. While your family story may be messy and without a God-guided vision, if you choose to identify yourself as seeking after God then you have the ultimate resource and can tune in guiding principles for your journey as a family. By tuning in, telling, and celebrating your family story, you can transform what is now ambiguous, subjective, and hopelessly messy into what is vivid, highly defined, and unique. By acquiring some tools for living out your God-guided vision, your family story, while still messy, will also tell and live the story of God for the world.

In tuning in your family vision, you are defining and shaping your story. With a family vision, you can consistently make wise decisions that align your own messy story with the unfolding high definition story of God for the world.

Why Make the Journey?

Living out your vision usually isn't easy. Jesus didn't say following him would be. However, on your journey you will come to accept your own messy family story and weave it into the unfolding story of God for the world.

Your character will be continually shaped more like Jesus', you will contribute to others becoming more like Jesus, and donate more and more love to a world that is hungry and thirsty for this kind of love.

You'll see and reach your highest potential, achieve greater freedom and clarity, and draw closer to each other, God, and those whom you encounter on your journey. You'll find an easier and clearer parenting task, cultivate leadership in all family members, create an energized family culture and realize family dreams.

Involve Your Family Now

Because this is an important family journey, I suggest that you commit to making it together. The more family members participate, the more powerful the transformation will be. However, perhaps not everyone is ready to commit to exploring and getting started. If that's the case, I want to encourage you to be sensitive to them, to gather those who are willing and to get started on the journey today.

If you have very young children, their commitment will take a different form from that of teens and adults. For those who are able, as a family:

- Commit together to the high definition journey
- Read the book together (or the adults read the book and the children join in at the *Family Journey Points*, below)
- Explore through the *Family Journey Point* section at the end of each chapter together
- Involve all members in each part of the journey

Be sure to go slowly. The time invested with each other and the process will pay huge dividends. Especially while tuning in your vision, the process is just as important as the results. Most often, going slowly will actually lead to faster and better results. Going fast will actually limit your growth potential and lead to slower and lesser results. Encourage each family member to track with the others in the process outlined in each session.

Because the journey involves powerful change, you may encounter some resistance. Use your judgment about how much to encourage participation in the journey. Again, go slow. Back off if a member or members are not yet open to exploring the high definition journey. Pushing those who are resistant will most likely backfire.

Approaching resistant family members with understanding and patience rather than judgment may open the door to the high definition journey for them in the future. Persevering in a humble, loving and sensitive way toward exploring and then committing together will pay off eternally.

Family Journey Point: Chapter One

To Ponder: *What are some of the stories of your family journey?*

To Consider: *Commit together to tuning in, celebrating, and telling your own family story.*

To Remember: *"I will make your name great, and you will be a blessing."*
Genesis 12:1-2 (NIV)

It All Begins With God

While Jesus was still talking to the crowd, his mother and brothers stood outside. They wanted to speak to him. Someone told him, "Your mother and brothers are standing outside. They want to speak to you." Jesus replied to him, "Who is my mother? And who are my brothers?" Jesus pointed to his disciples. He said, "Here is my mother! Here are my brothers! Anyone who does what my Father in heaven wants is my brother or sister or mother."

Matthew 12:46-50 (NIRV)

"Who is the leader of our family?"

Janet, her husband John, and their two daughters, eight-year-old Audrey and seven-year-old Libby, live in an urban neighborhood. They and their neighbors had noticed a van with a small beat-up camper trailer parked at the end of the block. The van had now been there five months.

Coming home from church one Sunday, Janet felt God gently leading her, "Go to the trailer and invite the people in the trailer to lunch."

Janet said, "John, I think we should invite whoever is in the trailer to lunch. I get the sense God is leading us to do this!"

"You can knock on the door!" replied John.

"You've got to come with me!" Janet pleaded.

"I'll come but you knock!" said John.

That afternoon, filled with adventure, they walked to the

trailer. Janet knocked on the door. Nothing. Then they heard a small voice. A woman opened the door a crack.

Janet, holding a shopping list in hand, said, "Hi, we're going to the store and wondered if we could pick anything up for you."

The woman seemed startled at having a visitor. "The only thing I have on my list is butter," she quietly replied.

By now the door had opened a bit wider. Janet, John, and their daughters could see that the woman was pregnant. A man and a two-year-old boy were also inside.

Janet asked, "Do you need bread?"

"Okay," replied the woman.

Janet, enjoying their encounter said, "Great. On our way home we'll stop by . . . We actually have a pot of stew on the stove too. Would you like to join us for lunch?"

"Sure," replied the woman.

Janet said, "Good—when we get back we can all walk together to our house over there."

Excitedly, Janet, John, and the girls walked to the store, the girls hopping and skipping every other step along the way. They were giddy with what God was doing with them that moment, as they took action and walked a journey only He could lead.[4]

Whatever your family circumstances, God wants to lead you on your own unique path of love. This path creates powerful meaning in your life. God wants you to make wise choices for your own circumstances that reflect the wisdom of God. God wants to guide you in tuning in a vision for your journey and wants to lead and inspire you all along the way.

We all know our own family story can be messy. The messiness of your story may be about:

- Abuse or addiction
- Flaring tempers that let anger get the better of you
- Infidelity or mistrust
- Difficulty communicationg needs or feeling understood
- Feeling guilty because you cannot live up to standards, either yours or others'
- Being stuck deep in debt
- Wanting to be part of a bigger story but feeling stuck in a smaller story

Without a bigger vision that only God can guide, you become defined by your messy family history and the messy world you live in. Who is your family's guide and leader? Perhaps you trust God to lead your life. What would it be like to trust God to lead your family? It takes commitment, an understanding of God's larger purpose, and faith to hand the leadership of your family to God. When you take this step, know you will have taken an important step of faith in committing your family to being an active partner with God. You will have made a high definition choice.

What if you were clear, intentional, and upfront about God being at the center of your family, and letting God lead? What if instead of just hoping God is or will be the leader of each family member's life, you made a clear commitment together to be accountable with each other by God's leadership?

You want the leader of your family to be someone who loves unconditionally, knows each member well, and desires the best for them. You want someone who is always present, even in the worst of times, and yet who will confront bad behavior. You want a leader who transforms the family and each individual member, speaks truthfully, and sees, embodies and empowers a vision for your family.

Does this sound like someone you know (*or would like to know*)? What if your family were accountable to God and together were consciously and intentionally inspired and led by God? If God were your family's leader then *you* would not be the leader. You and each member would serve at different times in the role of *a* leader with tremendous responsibility, but not as *the* leader of your family.

What if every family member not only enjoyed a relationship with God but was part of a dynamic family culture: living, breathing, playing and laughing with God as the leader and as a member of the family? You would be the kind of family Jesus is talking about when he says his mother and brothers (and family) are those who put what God wants ahead of what they want, who know it's not about them but about God.

Notice that Jesus gestures to his disciples and says that all who do what God wants—who obey God—are his family members. He's saying obedience is thicker than blood. He isn't saying his mother and brothers are disobedient and are not members of his family. He's rather raising obedience above blood as a definition of his family. So can you and your family.

What, then, does Jesus mean by "*all who do what God wants—who obey God—are his family members*?" If he means you are to obey so that you are acceptable to him, then you have a lot of work to do and can rightly feel anxious about earning Jesus' acceptance and membership into his family. The Bible says Jesus' standards are pretty high – perfectly high, in fact.[5] If this is what Jesus means then his good news is not good news at all.

If Jesus means, instead, for you to accept his gift of membership in the forever family of God, then you have no work to do at all but to accept what is before you this moment. Then you have the gift of being part of God's forever family. And your motivation for obeying God is your gladness and gratitude at enjoying such closeness with God and your brothers and sisters of God.

Think it through. If your goal is to follow God, it's just good sense to make God the leader of your family. A key to wanting and doing what God wants is to choose God to lead your family and continually be aligning your family's behaviors and values with what God wants. When you make this choice, know that you will have taken a step of faith. You will have taken the most important step in your journey.

Finding Our Way Out of the *What God Wants* Quagmire

The usual approach to finding what God wants begins with the assumption that God has in mind for us one and only one correct choice for every decision we face. When we go to the car lot to buy a new car, this approach says, there is one and only one vehicle God wants us to buy. All the others are second-best. While this traditional way has some wisdom within it about being sensitive to subtle nuances and mystery of God and God's guidance, it just isn't biblical.

The first trouble with this approach to seeking what God wants is that the Bible passages used to justify it have more to do with God's general, not specific, guidance for our lives. The passages cited are more about what to believe and how to live than about what God separately wants for each individual.[6]

The second trouble with this approach is that it avoids the freedom God wants for us. This approach has us no longer making decisions but pleading for God to tell us what to do. It asks God to attach, hold, and pull imaginary strings connected to our brain, hands, arms, heart, and legs as though we were a puppet at every whim and twitch of God. It would have us plead for God to tell us what to do every moment, rather than ask God for help in making responsible decisions.

The third trouble with this approach is that it's of little use in everyday decision-making. Would I lay stock still until God tells me which side of the bed to get out of? Or, would I camp out in the supermarket until I know which toothpaste God is having me buy? Is God saying, in essence, "*I will stream text messages to you with what to say, do, and think*" or is God saying, "*I provide my guidance, presence, and wisdom so that you can make wise decisions that honor me*?"

The fourth trouble is that it tends to promote immaturity in decision-making. A man deciding whom to marry decides that whichever girl calls him first is the one he is supposed to marry. We are tempted to assign meaning where none is intended. While the Bible *does* tell us to be child-like in our reliance upon God it *also* tells us to be wise and make wise decisions.[7] God wants to transform, encourage, and shape our character, mind, and thoughts so as to grow more and more mature.[8]

The fifth trouble is that it doesn't explain or deal with equal options. If two options are equal, why do we insist that God has only one in mind? Couldn't either one be an instrumental part of our journey of expressing the unfolding story of God?

The sixth trouble is that it often results in uncertain guidance. Seeking and waiting for God's guidance in the form of our own mysterious inner experience of God can result in uncertainty and frustration. Mystery is profoundly part of our journey with God but isn't God capable of communicating clearly with us?

With this uncertainty also comes the temptation to manipulate the decision-making process. A family member using this approach could be tempted to falsely boost their own position with a divine rubber-stamp by saying, "God revealed this to me."

The seventh trouble with this approach is that it promotes anxiety and guilt over missing the one-and-only thing God wants for every decision we face. Instead of feeling grateful for multiple opportunities we fret that we will miss the dot that is the center of what God wants for us. We feel as though we've been left behind, relegated to forever living a plan-B life because we missed the elusive Plan A.

I do not mean to ridicule those who hold to this way but honor them in our common journey of seeking after God's guidance. I expect that I can learn from everyone's insights and perspective, including theirs. Still, I don't believe the position is warranted that God has one and only one option that we must not miss.

Is There a Better Way?

God may offer you a specific message of guidance, but you do not need it to make a wise decision pleasing to God. If God does offer a specific message be glad and grateful and apply God's special message in making a wise decision. If God does not offer a specific message, be glad and grateful and rely upon the guidance God *is* providing.

If one family member says, "*God revealed this to me*," then be sure to ask them to define and explain their revelation. Then ask the family if it is comfortable with receiving what the member says as a revelation. If the revelation is not from God, then you will find the member is hiding behind what they say by cloaking their statement with a false authority. If the revelation is from God, then the tuning in process will prove it true.

God's guidance for making wise decisions comes to us through God's presence within us, the Bible, wise counselors, wisdom, common sense, our personal desire, and our past and present circumstances. What we're seeking is not so much an elusive dot representing what is God's one and only will for our family but rather a wise decision from among a number of alternatives. Therefore, I want to suggest a more Biblical and better question to ask: *How can we make a wise decision that honors God?*

If God Were the Leader of Your Family

If God were the leader of your family God would empower your tuning in your family vision by his presence within each member. Jesus says to those who follow him, "*the realm of God is within you.*"[9] He would show you what God wants. He would love you unconditionally. Yet he also would confront attitudes and behaviors alienating you from him. He would guide you, challenge you, provide for you, shape you, and transform you. He knows you and your messy family story and would weave your story with his. Your family would move, messy story and all, with clarity and vividness with God's movement for the world.

At first having God as your family's leader might seem awkward as you seek to trust God's leadership together. You might not be used to following, let alone trusting, a leader other than yourself to lead your family. This is especially true if other leaders in your life—parents, teachers, mentors—have not been trustworthy. For families with young children, trying to maintain some semblance of order and function, let alone to allow God to lead your family, might seem overwhelming. For couples, having a new leader and third partner might at first seem intrusive and disruptive. For families who feel discounted or outside the circle of the acceptance of others, having a lead partner who simultaneously loves you unconditionally and commands obedience may be radically new.

Sometimes we find ourselves negotiating with God. Consider the man in the story who tests the reality of God's presence and leadership in his life by praying,

> *"Lord, I promise if you will help me find a parking space, I'll attend worship every single Sunday all year!" Just then he spots a space opening up in front of him and says, "Never mind, Lord I just found one."*[10]

For families who feel settled in their faith journey, the idea of consciously and intentionally accepting God as the leader of the family may seem contrived, unnecessary or perhaps too risky. God, however, knows where you are and knows you well. God wants to lead not just your life but your family's. The best way to do this is to commit as a family to letting God lead. You will be delighted at God's leadership and be challenged and stretched in every way.

Even if you suspect that with God as your leader your family would be disjointed, unproductive and out of sync, why don't you let God lead for a while and see what happens? I think you will be surprised.

If you choose to have God as the leader of your family, each family member–whether man, woman or child–will stand equally before him, focused on him and accountable to him and God's visionary leadership. If you choose to have God as your leader, you reinforce to each other, especially to children, that God is a dynamic ever-present guide for life. To be sure, children are still *children* who rely upon their parents for support, protection, security, nurture, and to model wise and loving behavior, encouragement, and love.

Having God interact with your family story and lead your journey will not necessarily lead to an easier life. The journey involves discomfort, struggle, conflict, and suffering, along with transformed lives, healing, affirmation, transparency, new relationships, wholeness and unlimited reserves of love.

The high definition choice is not a one-time decision. You face this choice with every breath you take, word you utter, thought you think, and action you take. Whether as a parent, spouse, partner, child, or neighbor, you have the high definition choice concerning the words you use, the friendships you form, the thoughts you think, and how you spend your money and your time.

This choice is a choice for obediently participating with God within yourself and within your family in God's movement for the world. It is the choice for going with God wherever God leads. It could even be right down the street, like for Jan and Bill and their two daughters knocking on the door of the tiny camper trailer.

Even if you've individually been connected in some way with God, you are presented with a choice to involve your family in ways you may not have experienced before.

You can dynamically tune in and live a new and higher definition of being a family because God wants you to entrust God to lead your family on a journey of a lifetime. You will experience a whole paradigm-shift for being family. Your family will develop new leaders and leadership skills and cultivate spiritual growth. Your family can experience deep, loving, forgiving, transparent, and nurturing relationships with each other and with God. You will befriend others and donate this same love in every sphere of influence you choose. Your messy family story can reflect, tell, and live out God's story. All because God wants to lead your family in God's unfolding story for the world.

Family Journey Point: Chapter Two

To Ponder: *I define "leader," without using the word "lead" or "leader." as...*

To Consider: *Commit together to having God lead your family on this journey*

To Remember: *Jesus: "Anyone who does what my Father in heaven wants is my brother or sister or mother"*
Matthew 12:50 (NIRV)

Choosing to be Transformed

The Lord *is my light and my salvation—so why should I be afraid? The* Lord *is my fortress, protecting me from danger, so why should I tremble?*

Psalm 27:1 (NLT)

"But where's God when we're stuck?"

I drove the family station wagon from Dayton, Ohio to Cragsmoor, New York via Newburgh along the Hudson River to attend a family reunion. With me were my children, ages 11, 8 and 6 and our suitcases. I was pregnant with child number four. My husband would take a flight to join us later to minimize the time he needed to be gone from work.

As we approached the entrance to the New York Thruway, I felt a "nudge" tell me to stop here to fill the gas tank. I didn't react fast enough and told myself, "I'll stop at the next gas station." I never did encounter a gas station on the Thruway. After driving 45 minutes further the car's engine began to sputter. I realized we were out of gas.

Instead of just pulling over I prayed, "Oh Lord, can we please drive on a little farther? There doesn't seem to be any help here." The engine caught again so I kept on driving. Again the engine sputtered but I prayed, "Lord, there is no help here," and the engine caught again and I drove on for a short way. When the engine again sputtered, I pulled over and thought, "Thank you Lord. This is the third time the car gas gauge has shown empty so I'll just pull over and not try to stretch it out any more."

It dawned on me that I really needed help. My young children and my pregnant self could not realistically expect to walk for miles, if that's what it would take to get some gas for the car and walk back again.

Just then I looked across the divided highway. There stood a policeman giving a citation to a driver. I told the children to wait in the car for me, got out, waited for a break in the traffic, and then ran to the center island. I called out to the policeman, "I need some help!" He came to the center divide and I told him my situation. He agreed he would send someone with a gasoline can to my location. I thanked him and returned to the children.

Soon help arrived and a driver in a small pick-up truck pulled off the road behind us. He walked toward us carrying a gas can. I got out and greeted him. He gave us the gas. I paid him and thanked him heartily.

Pulling back out into traffic on the New York Thruway, I sighed, "Thank you Lord." Even when we make the foolish choice, I realized, the Lord's compassion and protection does not leave us without the aid we need.[11]

You have likely felt stuck in one way or another and experienced the messiness of life. You have experienced pain in your life in one way or another. Perhaps you have:

- Suffered the death of a loved one?
- Suffered a traumatic accident?
- Found yourself in a dead-end job?
- Experienced a stagnant marriage?
- Suffered from post-tramatic stress disorder?
- Used drugs or alcohol as an escape?
- Carried large financial debt?
- Experienced domestic violence?
- Carried pain like a deep bruise within you?

However you may have experienced it, you have felt stuck and have felt pain or hurt in some way.

Where's God When We're Stuck?

Without God providing the opportunity and choice for transformation and the family accepting it, the family struggles and never reaches its potential.

Where is God when we're feeling stuck? While God sometimes seems far away—especially when we feel stuck—God is present in the middle of the muck of our circumstance and pain. God knows and feels your pain and consistently speaks good news into your bad news situation. He consistently offers light into your darkness. He provides perspective, protection, power, and the wherewithal to persevere and be transformed as a family.

God Brings Perspective

When God says, "*I give your family My light and salvation,*" you have a new and eternal perspective on your painful circumstance and your family's potential. This perspective is not merely a possibility or a potential reality but a truth: when you accept God's offer to you of leadership you experience life-giving definition as a family. This new perspective does not begin when you die. You have eternal life when you accept God's offer, not a moment later. You *have* eternal life and, therefore, your perspective can be eternal. This is not to make your struggles small but rather to declare how big God is who loves you and the gift God daily and eternally provides you.

When you take a God-centered view you get a God-centered perspective about every family crisis, difficulty or opportunity. You allow God's light to shine on your pathway as a family. The size of your problem is brought into perspective as a mere splinter on the yardstick of eternal life. This perspective does not make your pain any less painful but frees your family to creatively think, brainstorm, network, and resolve your painful circumstance. You please God when you use all the resources God brings to bear into your circumstance.

> *One woman in her 50s was suffering from cancer. Doctors told her she had a year to live. The way she handled the traumatic circumstances of her disease was inspiring. She said, "I realize the urgency of the time I have left and I want to use it to help others and to let God be the leader of what's going on with me." While she clearly was grieving she also had an eternal perspective and others could see it so clearly it drew powerful attention to the God of her faith.*

God Brings Protection

Your family's source of security is God. God is your fortress, your armor of protection. The Bible says God is your shield, your helmet, your sword.[12] This doesn't mean bad things won't happen. It means that God will be with you as you choose how to respond.

Life on Earth is fragile. As the experience of September 11, 2001 so tragically and vividly demonstrated, we live in a broken world. Your life on this planet may be taken at any time. In the case of September 11, more than three thousand lives were taken. Millions of others were affected because of evil choices made by those who flew airplanes into large buildings.

God's love for every person on Earth is so great that God gave—and gives—utter freedom of choice for our behaviors, relationships, thoughts, and desires. God also hopes that each of us will one day choose to return to our Creator God and to keep on reaffirming our choice. This is an infinitely great love, this love God expresses.

This love is not a limited love where the god says, "I'll limit your freedom and your choices so I can protect you and lower my risk of you never returning to me." God's love is so great, so complete, and so full of risk that it is as though God tosses the family car keys to us and says, "Why don't you take the car tonight? Enjoy!" God does not say, "Hey, better safe than sorry. Here's a little Hot Wheels® car; you can play with it here at my feet rather than risk danger. No telling what could happen out there. And you'll never leave me and I won't have to worry about whether you'll want to return."

Because this is a messy, broken world in which life is precarious and fragile, the unfolding story of God on Earth is urgent and the choices we make are important. Where does God's protection fit into all this?

The shield God provides you for protection is love, the very same love that grants you utter freedom of choice. This love will not eliminate suffering from your life but will provide you with hope, healing, faith, and an ultimate life-giving well of water from which to draw.

The Bible says, "*keep on taking up the shield of faith*," or keep on choosing to accept and load up on God's love for you and for all in the form of what Jesus has done for you upon the cross ("the helmet of salvation").[13] The word "take" in the original Greek is a participle which we can properly translate as, "keep on taking." God wants you to keep on keeping on: to renew every day, your family's commitment to participating with God.

In addition, the Bible says, "*Take up ... the sword of the Spirit, which is the word of God.*"[14] God provides the message and words of the Bible as a means for encountering and participating with God as you reflect, memorize, recite, and act upon them. Put on the full armor of God as a family. Just as the family stuck on the New York Thruway began to rely on and experience the armor—the protection—of God, so can you.

You don't know how long your life on Earth will last but you can choose how you will live it and whose protection your family will trust.

God Brings Power

God is powerful and undefeated. God has a perfect record. God wants your family to partner with God. When you allow God to not only lead your *life* but also your *family* then your family has the power within it to overcome any obstacle, circumstance, or trouble.

When we feel stuck, our problems have power over us; they loom large in our lives. Yet, God is bigger than these problems with their power bearing down upon us. When God becomes the leader of your family then the presence and power of God resides within you all.[15] Though a mighty army surrounds you, you will not fall![16] The power within you now is greater than the power outside of you. There is nothing you cannot overcome or see through.

When you allow God to lead your life, the image of God within you is rekindled and reconnected with its source and the presence and power of God is now within you. The Bible says, "I stand at the door and knock. If anyone hears my voice and opens the door, I will come in and dine with him, and he with me."[17] When you allow God to lead your family, you open the door to God's leadership. The power of God is now at work within your family. The power within your family is now greater than the power outside you and any obstacle or difficulty you may face.

Your family now has the power, even in the face of great difficulty–illness, abuse, addiction, injustice, trauma or persecution–to freely choose its behavior and mode of being and to tune in its vision and live it out.

God Brings Perseverance

You can persevere through even the most difficult of family circumstances, through the most difficult of pains, troubles and sorrows, and the biggest of challenges. God gives us the best of both worlds when it comes to difficult times in our lives: power and guidance for persevering *and* reassurance about our future as part of God's forever family.

God says, "*I give your family my light and my salvation.*" God doesn't slap your hands as they reach for the cookie jar of God's goodness and say, "Just one! Take one or the other—my light or my salvation—but not both! No taking too many cookies out of my cookie jar!" No, they come together. You can't have one without the other.

If you have light and not salvation what good is that (and God *is* good)? Imagine you are a family not yet knowing and relating with God and I offer you a self-help suggestion. All it can do is help. But it can't save your family ship from sinking. Re-arranging the deck chairs on the Titanic won't do it. But you already know that.

On the other hand, if you have salvation but no light, how can you see well enough to partner with God in what God is doing in the world? God wants your family to be a citizen of heaven on Earth, partnering with God, not sitting passively through life waiting to be transformed into a citizen of heaven after you die.

God's light can shine into the midst of your family's struggle so that you can be transformed, see your challenge, adapt your plan and behavior, and persevere in using your painful circumstance for the benefit of God's unfolding story for the world.

Family Journey Point: Chapter Three

To Ponder: What would it be like to know that the power of God's love is inside of you and available for overcoming any challenge you face?

To Consider: Pray aloud together something like this: *God, welcome to our home and our family. You are bigger than any problem we face. We gladly invite You to be inside each one of us. In Jesus' name – thank you God!*

To Remember: *"The Lord is my light and my salvation – so why should I be afraid? The Lord is my fortress, protecting me from danger, so why should I tremble?"*

Psalm 27:1 (NLT)

Principle #2: Self-Awareness

When they had (let down their nets), they caught such a large number of fish that their nets began to break. So they signaled their partners in the other boat to come and help them, and they came and filled both boats so full that they began to sink. When Simon Peter saw this, he fell at Jesus' knees and said, "Go away from me, Lord; I am a sinful man!"

— **Luke 5:6-8** (NIV)

Your Family

". . . Go home to your family and tell them how much the Lord has done for you, and how he has had mercy on you."

Mark 5:19 (NIV)

"Who is our family?"

On a flight to Kansas, a woman in her mid-seventies sat next to me. Her daughter, son-in-law, granddaughter and grandson walked past her along the aisle. She explained that she was traveling with her grandkids competing in a national track meet. Her granddaughter was a nationally top-ranked junior runner. She showed me a news article about her granddaughter. Her daughter had been a competitive long-distance runner. Her son-in-law was also a runner. All of them except the grandmother, who had recently suffered an injury, were still active runners.

I asked her, "So how is it that through the generations this is such a big part of your lives?"

With a glimmer in her eye, she proudly smiled and said, "That's just who we are and what we do. Running is at our core."

Just as you are a unique person, your family is a unique family. Because you are a unique family, exploring answers to the question, "*Who are we?*" will bring unique results. Each member of your family shapes who you are as a family, uniquely adding to the whole. You each play a role within your family. In this way, you each are intricately connected with each other.

You are part of your family for a reason. Yet if you change any aspect of your self or any other member, then the whole of your family shifts or changes. When one of you changes, grows, moves out, or is transformed, then your whole family is changed. For example, if one family member quits smoking, begins a new personal habit of praying, joins a small group, or commits to no longer telling "little white lies" then the whole family is affected.

The family and friends of the man who called himself "*Legion*" were changed. Legion suffered under the power of a violent and deranging illness, driving him to live amongst dark hillside tombs. When Jesus healed him he was transformed, and so was everyone around him, as they saw his transformation and heard about Jesus' healing power.[18]

Who you are is shaped also by where you've been. Specifically, the baggage, both good and bad, that adults and children bring to the family, deeply shapes how the family behaves. Who Legion had become was profoundly shaped by where he had been—the seemingly unbearable condition from which he was healed.

Legion was a man described by Luke as under the power of "an unclean spirit" and who, it seems, behaved and lived the part. He would shriek and scream and carry on, beating, bruising, and cutting himself upon the stones he lived among. Others who had tried to subdue him were no longer able to do so. They were defeated by the power of what ailed the man: He broke free from the chains they'd shackled him in. While Luke doesn't say, I wonder if those who intervened were family? Or if they weren't family did they become like family, as close friends of family often become? If not by blood then by sweat in the efforts they made in their attempts to intervene in his tragic self-mutilation.

After his encounter with Jesus, this same man returned to his hometown, including to his family and friends, and expressed and embodied the transformation brought about by Jesus' compassion. Legion wanted to go into the broader world and travel with Jesus, to literally follow him. But Jesus insisted that he stay and share all that Jesus had done for him with those who were most aware of who he had dramatically been.

Jesus knew that Legion would have his greatest *initial* impact upon those folks and not anyone else. Of course, as the years and centuries have gone by, he has affected—through his messy family story woven into the unfolding story of God—even such folks as you and I.

As a family that has chosen God as its leader, you each have within you the presence, image, and power of God to be the family God intends you to be.

Family Luggage
"What's in my luggage?"

You carry within you traits and habits that you learned as you grew up—your luggage. The contents might be what are usually perceived as good habits, like honesty, love, leadership capability, conflict management skills, good stewardship, intelligence, humility, confidence, and so on. On the flip side are habits like dishonesty, ignorance, hatred, disloyalty, addiction, complacency, and so on.

These habits are influenced by the experiences of your upbringing and your perception of them. How aware you are of your luggage plays an important role in your continuing growth into the image of God. The more aware you are of the luggage you carry from your upbringing, the more informed and free you will be in the choices you face in life today.

As an example, suppose your parents' behavior was frequently combative and harmful when in conflict. Their behavior might then have taught you an unhealthy way of handling conflict. You might then carry the luggage of this behavior when you experience conflict. Or, in saying, "I don't want to be like mom and dad," you might then carry the luggage of being overly passive in conflict.

On the positive side, suppose your parents' behavior impressed in you the virtue of persevering in the face of personal challenges. Because they modeled effective behavior in the face of hardship, you might then often be in a position to effectively face difficult challenges in your own life.

When you are not aware of luggage you carry within you, the luggage often shows up when you least need it or want it. It can be like an old smelly tennis shoe. It's good for tossing around in the back yard playing fetch with your dog but as foot apparel for a date with your loved one, it is inappropriate, consistently under-performs and stinks. By becoming aware of your luggage, you inform the choices you make about your relationships, communication and behavior.

How did your parents treat you? What did they say to you? Did they use judgmental language ("Good girl!" "Bad girl!")? Moralistic language? ("You should be a good boy for me"). Encouraging language? ("Nice job!" "You can feel good about what you have done!").

What were your parents' beliefs? What was their world-view? What were their values? What were they enthusiastic about? What did they disapprove of? How did they handle conflict between themselves? How did they handle conflict with you?

Parenting is a foundational responsibility. Parents provide not only the child's genetics but also the environment within which their children grow into adulthood. Parents influence attitude, perspective, world-view, behavior, faith-development, spirituality, education, health, well-being, curiosity, self-esteem. Parents are the primary packers of their child's luggage for the trip called life. By taking a mental inventory of how your parents' behavior influences and shapes you, you can be more informed in the choices you make about your behavior, relationships, communication, beliefs, and values.

Others who may influence you in the contents of your luggage are your siblings, extended family, schoolmates, coaches, teammates, pastors, teachers and other influential adults.

The Family Whispers
"Why do we face the same problems again and again?"

Gavin Stevens, a character in William Faulkner's play, ***Requiem for a Nun***, says, "*The past is never dead. It's not even past.*"[19] Your luggage hangs around. The Bible says we often do not do the good that we want to do and instead do what is ingrained within us.[20] Our old luggage seems forever in the attic of our lives, ready to be discovered or used, by default. As a result, unless we unpack our negative luggage, the same problems occur again and again. Even when we buy new luggage, the old is stashed in the wings in case the new one fails or is forgotten.

In coaching families I have often referred to this phenomenon as the *family whispers*. As you go about your day, your family whispers into your inner-ear the powerful messages from your past that influence you today. They aren't necessarily voices that you hear, though some may forever recall a parent's voice from the past as though they were speaking it aloud today. These whispers, if they're not voices you hear, are subconscious assumptions you make about what is normal for you. They are perceptions you have of your parents' or guardians' behavior and your experiences growing up. The whispers are messages you know and live by. Whispers can be positive or negative in their impact upon you. They influence you powerfully. You might not be consciously aware of the whispers but they follow you all the same.

Typically, the whispers consist of a dozen or so of these messages, some bearing greater influence than others. Here are a few examples, both positive and negative:

- You will never amount to much
- There is only so much to go around in this world
- Your worth is based on what you do
- Your worth is based on who you are
- Your worth is based on how much you do
- Your worth is based on how well you do what you do
- God cannot/can be trusted
- Sexuality is/is not good
- Drugs are the best fix for what ails you

What can you do about your luggage?

Is the past never past or can you overcome your luggage? Your luggage is like the monster in a horror movie. No matter what you do, he keeps coming back. You feel fortunate that the movie ended and the bad guy died, but worn out by the fact that his death didn't happen until just before the credits rolled. You can overcome your luggage, here a little, there a little, through the healing work of God in you, becoming ever more informed and free in every choice you face. As a fellow-journeyer, let me offer some suggestions.

(1) Explore the contents of your luggage

Become aware of the influences of your past upon your present reality. When you discover positive pieces of luggage—affirm them again and again and share their value with others as often as you think others might benefit. Positive luggage is a gift you continue to unwrap as you affirm the positive habit and use it in relationship with others.

Identify negative luggage, behaviors that are ineffective, that you find difficult to change, and that often result in misunderstandings and feelings of frustration or anger. Often, it will take someone else, usually a loved one, confronting you about your behavior for you to understand that you are carrying negative luggage. They might not think of your behavior as negative luggage, but they will know your behavior causes them problems and is ineffective.

Here's an example: One of the pieces of negative luggage I assumed was the message, "*Do not make waves—avoid conflict at all costs. Conflict is not good.*" When I was confronted with personal conflict I thought I had somehow failed and felt guilty. I was quite adept, an expert even, at resolving other people's conflict. But when I was personally in conflict with another person, I ran. Fight or flight–I chose the first flight out of town. I didn't have the tools to work it out when my needs, principles, or desires were in direct conflict with someone else's, and to resolve the matter in a way that left both sides pleased by the result.

The strategies I used when confronted with personal conflict, were ineffective and reinforced what the whisper—my negative luggage—was saying. As I matured and trained for pastoral ministry, I became aware of this negative luggage and committed to making different choices when confronted with this conflict. However, it wasn't until I met my wife Heidi that I more effectively discovered specific new behavior choices and attitudes concerning personal conflict. I experienced a transformation. I now see conflict as an opportunity for growth, learning, and drawing closer to the other.

Resolving negative luggage can happen instantaneously, but more often takes years or, in some cases, your whole life's journey. As a result of wrestling with your negative luggage you may have opportunities throughout your life—like Legion did with his family and friends—to share with others the transformation you have experienced.

Whatever luggage you may carry, you can choose the ultimate source of transformation, God, to transform your character so that it more and more resembles the character of Jesus.

Talk with your loved one, or someone else you trust, about your behavior or communication choices. Explain your thought process as you find yourself in situations that you don't handle well. Ask them for suggestions about other behaviors or approaches that might be more effective.

(2) Acknowledge that you still carry your luggage

Owning up to the luggage you carry on your journey will position you to be open to transforming of this negative behavior through time. Admitting what you struggle with defangs the monster of your persisting negative habit, and moves you further along the road to positive behaviors. Others, if they are helpful in their behavior, will be more inclined to support you in seeking out transformation and new behaviors in place of persistent old ones. You may also encounter others who are reluctant for you to change and grow, for their own selfish reasons.

Even after you have explored your luggage and found effective alternative behaviors, you will need to continue to acknowledge your old negative luggage and its persistent nature. Acknowledging your old habits helps prevent you from falling back into the ingrained pattern of old behavior. You will be setting a clear boundary between what was and what now is, between the pattern of behavior you used to automatically fall into and your new effective and informed choice.

When it comes to the wrongdoing of others against you, the idea of *forgiving and forgetting* does not come from the Bible.[21] *Forgive and forget* comes from Shakespeare—King Lear, act four, scene seven.[22] If you forget about your negative luggage it will control your behavior. Sometimes forgiving means *remembering* the wrong done to you, while choosing to release the wrong-doer. Resolve, but do not forget, your past.

(3) Express gratitude and thanks for those whose behavior contributed to your positive luggage

Express gratitude to God and thanks to your parents and others for their contribution to any positive luggage that you gladly tap into.

(4) Commit to no longer carry your old negative luggage

Commit to no longer believing and no longer acting upon negative family whispers within you. Commit to stopping your old pattern of behavior. I committed to stop shutting down, tensing up, and feeling guilty when confronted with personal conflict. Write down your commitment.

> *I commit to... (no longer withdrawing, tensing up, and feeling guilty in the face of personal conflict).*

(5) Forgive those whose behavior contributed to your negative luggage

Forgive your parents and any others for their behavior that has added to any negative luggage you carry. Perhaps they were, like you are today, journeying toward a better way. Perhaps they did the best they could for their circumstances, the era in which they lived and for their maturity level and the support they had around them. Even if they didn't do the best they could, were immature, despised goodness, were irresponsible and behaved badly—forgive them. If you choose not to forgive them for their behavior, then you burrow more deeply within you the wound that began with their behavior. You invite bitterness that festers like an ulcer within your soul. You tie yourself more tightly to your dusty old luggage.

Your perception of others' behavior also plays a role in the negative luggage you carry. Your parents may have behaved reasonably and in a loving manner but your perception of their behavior resulted in the creation of negative luggage. Or your parents behaved badly and your faulty perception resulted in you perceiving insult beyond injury. If you are unsure whether you bear negative luggage because of your parents' behavior or because of your perception of their behavior, ask someone you trust, perhaps a capable friend, a pastor, or counselor, and discuss your experiences.

If your parents or the ones whose behavior contributed to your negative luggage are alive and you can safely approach them, express forgiveness to them in person. Before you forgive them you will need to provide details and explain what behavior caused you pain and how their behavior affected you. Or write a letter, tear it up (having aired out your pain) and write a second, more reasoned and dispassionate letter. Or, write a letter then burn it as a way of symbolizing forgiveness. Whichever way you forgive, do forgive and be sure to identify the specific behaviors that caused you pain.

Even if they are no longer living, forgive them.

> *Dad, Mom, (other) I love you and forgive you for... (specific behavior that contributed negative luggage). I felt (hurt, confused, bruised, belittled, disrespected, angry . . .) by your behavior. Your behavior influences me still today. While I will not forget the influence of your behavior upon me, I forgive you. And now I choose a new way.*

(6) Ask God for wisdom and for help.

If you want to experience transformation, go to the source. Talk with God. Admit that you are powerless to transform your behavior and ask for God's help in overcoming it. And, ask for wisdom in how to handle those situations you struggle with. Be open and sensitive to what God reveals to you.

(7) Commit to choosing your behavior despite the luggage you carry

You have explored and come to understand more about the contents of your luggage. You have expressed gratitude and thanks for positive luggage. You have committed to no longer behaving in your old negative luggage way. You have forgiven folks for their contribution to your negative luggage. You have admitted that you are powerless to transform your behavior and have asked God for help and wisdom. You are now ready to choose a new way, despite the influence of the negative luggage you carry. Choosing a new way often involves progress bit by bit, here a little, there a little.

Let others know what you are doing and enlist their support. As an example:

> *I have a problem addressing personal conflict. I have tended to run from conflict. Now I am choosing a new way to respond to personal conflict—with openness and courage, seeing opportunity for deeper relationship, desiring resolution and seeking the truth. I now use centering prayer to help me be open.*
>
> *I want you to be my reality check with the progress I am making. Will you be my accountability partner about my commitment to this new behavior?*

Write down, or journal about, your new commitment.

Keep on the journey

Ironically, the key to growing in our awareness of ourselves is to grow in our awareness of God. If you want to know yourself, get to know God. When I began using centering prayer, I became more aware of God in the midst of stressful conflict and so was able to remain relatively open and loving. It took me years to get to a place of truly allowing God to transform me in this way.

But strap yourself in because when you add a loved one's journey through the process of resolving negative luggage let the fun begin. It's like getting rid of the training wheels and, without dad running alongside with his grip on the bike, wobbling down the street alone for the first time.

The combination of your luggage with your loved one's luggage creates a whole new interactive dynamic. You can support your loved one by learning about their family and experiences growing up and becoming more aware of what behaviors trigger discomfort in your loved one.

When others speak with more energy, anger, frustration or other emotion than I believe a matter warrants then I begin to wonder why. I might say something like, "*You know, John, I respect your feeling of anger. I'm sensing a lot of energy and emotion coming from you on this issue than it seems to merit. I wonder what that's about*?" You may find that your behavior has triggered negative luggage within your loved one. Understanding each other's negative luggage will go a long way toward nurturing mutual support and being open to the transformative power of God at work in your family.

Seeing Your Family's Potential
"What's our potential?"

Your family has immense potential. Most families have not considered their potential. The Bible consistently says that what you think about is what you become.[23] You can be transformed by the renewing of your thoughts, by continually renewing what you think about.

When Jesus is the leader of your family, he will take you on an amazing journey. Your potential is limited only by your thoughts. As you expand your thoughts in following Jesus so will your potential expand.

Your journey with Jesus is interactive. As you make your way through one set of rapids and move around one bend in the river, Jesus leads you along into a new vista, a new set of opportunities for your family's journey together. In this way, your potential is not so much a photograph as it is a high definition movie. Rather than thinking of your potential as a goal, a number, or a status of accomplishment, consider your potential as a never-ending journey. The journey is about God's leadership for your family, God's relationship with you, and each of you with each other.

See your family at its best, yielding to God's leadership, full of God's presence within, transforming lives both within your family and out in the world. See your family seeking not to be good but to be God's. See your family passionate about what it is doing and enjoying being a family, part of God's forever family. See your family behaving and communicating in-step with the unfolding story of God for the world. See your family doing what it is fit to do, that would be impossible without the power and presence of God.

There are no limits or expectations about what your family's potential is. If God is the leader of your family, the only limit to your family's potential is that it cannot be contrary to what God is about. It cannot be contrary to unconditional love and to the presence, character, behavior, and person of Jesus.

Let me suggest to you that your potential is not necessarily about being successful but about being faithful. Your potential doesn't need to be loud and engender lots of attention. As you realize your potential through God's leadership, you will pique the interest and curiosity of others. Every family is different. As your family prays about its potential you may see long-range details or you may see more intermediate or even short-term details. Who better to ask about your family's potential than your family's leader?

> *Lord, what do you want us to see right now about our family's potential?*

Write down what you see. Explore together about what you see or even what you imagine. Be positive toward each other, not judging or squashing the comments of anyone. Let what is said be heard, understood, and reflected upon.

Potential is just that—*potential*. The moment that counts is now. That is the moment in which you journey. Why concern yourselves with your potential? Seeing your potential motivates you in this moment and propels you forward in the moments ahead. Seeing your potential realizes your potential. You will be transformed by the renewing of your minds as you see your family's potential. You will call into action every cell of your body, every thought, idea, and activity that realizes your potential.

You can celebrate the vast and beautiful potential you have as a family. You can trust your leader to lead you on your journey one moment at a time toward realizing and expressing your potential. *What a journey!*

Try this visioning exercise: It is three years from today. You are sitting with a long-lost friend in the shade of a large oak tree on a hillside overlooking your house. You feel a gentle warm breeze in your face. You are describing to your friend the remarkable journey you and your family have journeyed these last three years. What do you say?

Five years from today you meet again in the same place with the same gentle warm breeze upon your face. What do you say?

Ten years from today you meet again in the shade of the same oak tree. What do you say?

Describe your family as you imagine them interacting with each other in each of those time periods?

After completing the above, reflect on what you have said or written. How do your reflections strike you?

Fig. 1

Family Journey Point: Chapter Four

To Ponder: What do you like about your family? If you could change one thing about your family, what would you change?

To Consider: Pray aloud together: *Lord, what do you want us to see right now about our family's potential?*

To Remember: *"... Go home to your family and tell them how much the Lord has done for you, and how he has had mercy on you"*

Mark 5:19 (NIV)

The Family System Story

And he departed and began to publicly proclaim in (the region of the ten cities) how much Jesus had done for him, and all the people were astonished and marveled.

Mark 5:20 (AMP)

"Why Einstein was right"

Pilots had always fallen short of the objective of breaking the sound barrier. The closer they came the more the plane vibrated. Then Chuck Yeager said to himself, "Maybe once you get through, everything calms down," and sped up at the point where everyone else slowed down.

A mother heard her live-at-home son coming home late at night on days he had community college classes. Her anxiety increased. She tried everything she could to keep him functioning as a student, from serving him coffee in the morning to threatening to take his car keys in the evening. Her own stress increased, and her son seemed to feel more at ease in staying out late. Worried that she might have a son who flunks out of college, she was encouraged to get out of the triangle between herself, her son, and his irresponsible behavior. She was encouraged to shift the pain, by telling him (when he was not out late) as calmly as possible, "Son, I've been thinking things over (Mach 1). I have decided (Mach 2) that you have a right to stay out late and to enjoy life in the way you want, and to risk flunking out of college (Mach 3). After all, it's up to you (Mach 4).

I would like to stop nagging you, but I've got a problem. My sense is that you might soon fail your classes (Mach 5), based on your choice to stay out so late as often as you do (Mach 6). I don't want to be stuck with so much of the tuition and no degree to show for it, and having two other kids to see through college (Mach 7), so I'll make an agreement with you (Mach 8). I don't want you to keep on staying out so late and not getting the sleep and classwork you need because it hurts your education, everyone's finances, and yourself. Having said that, if you will agree to pay our portion of the tuition, I will agree to never mention your staying out late again (Mach 9)."[24]

Allowing God full reign as leader of your family is not an easy transition. The primary reason why is because every family has a system story that makes this transition seem either impossible or extremely difficult. The family system story is the continually repeating life story or world-view of the family. The system story that lies buried in the family's subconscious determines the behavior of the family no matter how they are organized.

One characteristic of the family system is where the family locates itself on the spectrum between control and permission-giving. For those families with parents, where on the spectrum do the parents choose to behave with respect to their children? For those families that are couples, where on the spectrum does the couple place itself as they interact with each other?

The table below is one way to think about a continuum between controlling behavior and permission-giving behavior.[25] The table shows the benefits of controlling behavior (upper left box) and of permission-giving (upper right box). The table also shows the draw-backs of each (lower left and lower right). Each family manages this tension between control and permission-giving by the decisions they make and their behavior. Usually their decisions and behaviors are consistent with their system story and always place them somewhere on this table.

Our Family's Environment:
Controlling or Permission-Giving?

+ Safety, protection, certainty, self-preservation, low risk **Behavior-Control**	+ Encourages learning, communication, innovation, creativity, responsibility, relationship-building, growth, freedom, positive motivation and focus; clarity of purpose and authority **Permission-Giving**
Controlling; stifling of growth, creativity, communication, and relationship-building; encourages fear-motivated behaviors, slow to respond to new opportunities; ambiguous purpose and authority -	Chaos, high risk, uncertainty -

Being a parent of young children, I recognize the importance of some level of control. But the Bible steers a course that encourages permission-giving and seeking the wisdom of God as we make decisions.[26] It recognizes that we will make bad choices but still indicates that we have the freedom to make choices anyway.

Permission-giving nurtures an environment where we each can take risks, be innovative, and think creatively. We are then free to use our gifts in timely response to an opportunity, and be faithful in using our own family story to tell and live the story of God for the world. Permission-giving requires that parents let go of trying to control their child and the results of their choices. If a child makes a bad decision, consider it a lesson learned.

Wherever you have placed yourself in the past between controlling and permission-giving, when you tune in your family vision and begin living it out you have created a whole new way of being. You introduce freedom with order, choices within limits, respect with firmness, all at the same time. You have a positive and principle-focused discipline.

The way your family behaves is a result of each member playing a particular role in the family. When one member's role shifts, as the mother of the college-aged son intentionally shifted away from her pain-bearing role, then the character, behavior, and expectations of the family itself shifts. Each family member is interdependent with the others. Each member is connected to, or can have her own effect upon, every other member. When considering your family, each member therefore operates as part of a larger whole and not in isolation. Each member functions according to their position in the organic network that is their family.

Looking at your family as a system is like seeing your family as a team or a body. When your head aches, your whole body carries the burden of the headache. In the same way, when one of your family members has a problem, all of your family members have a problem. Let's say your toddler begins to act out and regress in behavior. Knowing that you are a team means you understand not that your toddler is "*the sick one*" but that your toddler's behavior is a presenting problem. To resolve the problem you review your whole team. The toddler is the one in whom the family's stress has surfaced. You review every member's participating role and decide how to fit the pieces together differently so as to impact the presenting problem.

Your family is the team that you review, nurture, and look within for answers. Consider, for example, changing one or the other or both parents' schedules so that they can spend more time with their toddler and see if that resolves the presenting problem.

Interestingly, when God is your family's leader God becomes a member of your family system or team. That's encouraging news! Legion comes home a healed man. He is no longer dependent on his family members tying him down out on the hillsides to prevent him from hurting himself. He no longer plays the role of a dependent needy member. He is transformed by Jesus and takes on a new role of sharing with his family about what Jesus has done for him. His new role is evangelist and vision-caster for his family. And his family, relatives, and friends marvel and are astonished. His family will never be the same again.

What roles do you play within your family in relation to the other members? Realize that by shifting your role and your behavior, you challenge and shape the perspective, character, and behavior of each of the other family members. The family system story is a repeating story of behaviors and choices. Einstein said, "*Insanity is doing the same thing over and over again and expecting different results.*" He also said, "*The problems that exist in the world today cannot be solved by the level of thinking that created them.*"

Whether you are physically healed or not as a result of your relationship with God, you can experience a newfound freedom as a family that functions as an organic team with a common purpose. When you see your family as a unified team and commit to God's leadership for your family you can grow in your understanding of your family and how you can encourage your family in reaching its potential.

You will understand your family better and improve your ability to nurture your family's well-being. In the face of any challenge or opportunity, you can trust God to journey with you, to ease anxiety, to reassure and empower as you manage what might otherwise be stressful presenting problems. You can be wholly present with each other, God, and the presenting problem or opportunity. Ask questions of each other to better understand each other in the midst of stressful circumstances. Use humor with each other as a way to recognize that, despite the challenges you currently face, the goodness of God can prevail in every detail of your life.

Achieving results as a family

Insanity is doing the same thing over and over again and expecting different results. Expecting different results will not create different results. To expect your family to thrive simply because you *expect* them to is wishful thinking. That is like getting on a flight scheduled to go from Portland to San Francisco and expecting it to arrive in New York. My expectation will not change the fact that my flight will travel a southerly route and touch down on the runway in San Francisco. Only when my expectation matches reality will my expectation be met. Are your expectations important? Yes. But they are only one aspect of thriving as a high definition family.

What about positive thinking? If instead of *expecting* the flight to land in New York I *think positively* that the flight will land there I'm still dealing in folly. My positive thinking will not influence the fact that the flight arrives in San Francisco. Is positive thinking important? Yes. But it's only one aspect of thriving as a high definition family.

Will *hoping* that God will take over your life, giving you directions as though you were a puppet handled by a Master Puppeteer, result in your family thriving more fully? No. God is interested in the minute details of your life—the Bible says God knows the number of hairs on your head.[27] However, God is not interested in taking over your life but rather nurturing and empowering you to grow more and more into the character of God for the benefit of the world.

If thriving as a family isn't brought about by your expectations, positive thinking, or a hope that God will take over and make your difficult decisions for you, then what does bring about new and effective results for you as a family? What if you trust God and step out in an act of faith in following

God's leadership? What if you allow God to be the source of your transformation? What if you ask God for understanding and wisdom and to transform your family? If you choose to follow God's leadership then your responsibility is to commit again every day to this same leadership and guidance on your journey. Beware, however, that in trusting God, your behavior, thoughts, attitudes, and character will begin to change!

Legion received healing from Jesus then shared his transformation with family, relatives and friends (see Chapter 4). Taking Einstein's words one step further, I say: Insanity is continuing to rely on yourself and still expecting change to happen. Receive the transformative gift of God instead and, like Legion, apply yourself in light of the gift of God's leadership in your family. You will discover more about who you are as a family as you respond to God's leadership. Try on for size the way of unconditional love. Try on the principled truth of God revealed in the person of Jesus, and deeply discover who you are becoming as a family.

Family Journey Point: Chapter Five

To Ponder: Does everyone in your family at least occasionally have an opportunity to teach, serve, or entertain the rest of the family?

To Consider: Try on for size the way of unconditional love as modeled and empowered by Jesus. Totally accept and love everyone without exception for one week and see what happens.

To Remember: *"And Legion departed and began to publicly proclaim how much Jesus had done for him, and all the people were astonished and marveled."*

Mark 5:19 (NIV)

A Thriving Family

During the night Paul had a vision of a man of Macedonia standing and begging him, "Come over to Macedonia and help us." After Paul had seen the vision, we got ready at once to leave for Macedonia, concluding that God had called us to preach the gospel to them.

Acts 16:9-10 (NIV)

"How does a thriving family think and behave?"

A couple in their early 40's through their regular habit of prayer came to hear God saying, "If you make yourself available, I have things I can do with you!" So they set about becoming more free and available for God. They set about retiring early and re-imagining their story. They trusted God to guide them and to present them with opportunities to serve.

They thought about replacing missionaries on furlough, teaching, doing mission trips oversees, volunteering their time in various ways, and serving with others through their church.

At age 53, he was promoted to a position that paid relatively well. They resisted the temptation to buy a new house commensurate with his new position. They resisted buying the latest cars. They invested wisely. They began to wonder, "What would it take to really pull the plug?" and began to formulate a plan. He retired at age 58, she at 57.

They prayed about what might come next. Within a few months an opportunity came for them to participate with Medical Teams International on a trip to Haiti. They thought to themselves, "Hmmm, not sure where this all takes us but it's an adventure—yeah, let's go!"[28]

A thriving family is one that consistently donates love and embodies and expresses the unfolding story of God for the world. Paul, Timothy, and Silas picked up and moved to Macedonia because they sensed God's vision for them to express God's good news for the Macedonians.

If a thriving family were an apple tree it would bear lots of ripe, juicy apples. New apple trees would sprout nearby and, eventually, far and wide, that would themselves bear lots of new apple trees. Thriving families nurture, encourage, and inspire others who also allow their messy story to weave into God's unfolding story for the world.

A declining family, by contrast, moves only from crisis to crisis, inconsistently reacting to problems, living a lifestyle that changes depending on social trends, its current set of friends, and its own moods and whims. These families are often guided by egos and status.

A declining family has no guiding principles by which it lives except that its members should get and do what they want. These families have unclear—often unspoken—standards. For a declining family with children, the parents are not accountable to the family for their behavior and are not encouraged to be appropriately vulnerable with their children. The children are not taught or modeled effective leadership, self-discipline, and communication skills. The children are not provided a clear framework from which to experiment, learn, and mature. Their motivation comes not from within but from without in the form of rules and social acceptance. Parents apply rules randomly and inconsistently. The declining family may co-exist, for fear of conflict, with a fake harmony.

Faith is handled as though it were a secret, personal religion. God, if acknowledged at all, is kept at arms-length. If the declining family system were an apple tree, it might accidentally and occasionally produce an apple here or there.

Though a declining family system can express a stubborn will to survive, eventually the tree becomes a withered stump, destined to dissolve into the soil from which it sprang.

Five Skills of a Thriving Family

A thriving family will consistently, intentionally, and systematically go about building trust, mastering conflict, achieving unity, embracing mutuality, and focusing on principles.[29]

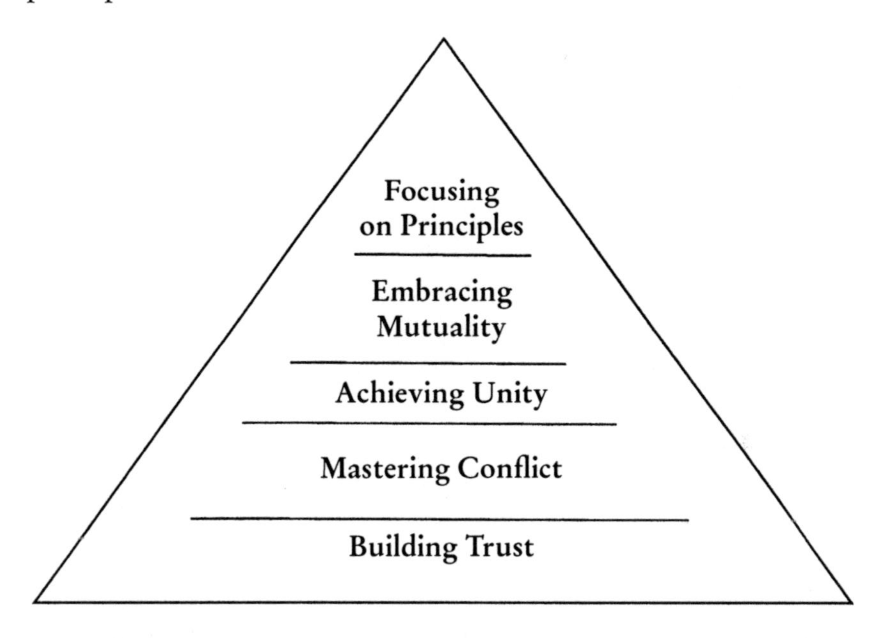

(1) Building trust

Trust is the most essential building block of a thriving family. Building trust is all about being open, vulnerable, and trustworthy. Trust isn't about predicting behavior, such as, "*I trust that my children will pick up their clothes on the floor this morning.*" This is about saying, "*I commit wholeheartedly to this journey wherever it may lead, even if the journey means that I will never be the same again, even if I experience deep pain and sacrifice mixed in with joy, exuberance, and ecstasy, because I am committed to the journey with you and with our leader.*"

Trust is about being vulnerable with each other and with God, laying bare your shortcomings, difficulties, gifts, opinions, ideas, and strengths and allowing God to lead your family. Being vulnerable with each other relies on each member being trustworthy, behaving in a way that elicits trust. If I say that I'll be on time picking up my children but consistently am not then I discourage their trust in me. They become less inclined to be vulnerable enough to expect that I'll arrive on time and become resentful as I expect them to be trustworthy when I myself am not modeling trustworthiness.

When Jesus is your leader you can follow his example. He exemplified trust and vulnerability, praying, for example, that he not have to face the monumental challenge of going to the cross and giving his life. He laid himself bare. Then he prayed, "*Creator God, not what I want but what you want. Let what you want be done within me.*"[30]

Trusting others is about saying things like, "*I made a mistake. I need help. You are more gifted than I at this—will you lead us in this exercise?*" Or, "*Please accept my apology for raising my voice at you in anger.*" Being a steward of each other's trust is about building each other up and encouraging each other to be reliable and faithful and not to inflict pain.

Building trust isn't just about spending time together. Some families have been together for many years but haven't built deep trust and may even actively mistrust each other. Some families can count on two hands the months they have been together and yet trust each other in profound and amazing ways.

Consider the example of Lydia. Jesus continues to invite folks to come to him and see what he's about. He invites people to have the courage to follow him. When Lydia listened to Paul about following Jesus, she committed her life and her resources to trusting Jesus and then to leading a new outpost of followers in Philippi, all within a month. The key to building trust is courage and being trustworthy. You must have the courage to let your guard down together and to let go of whatever will happen next! You must be trustworthy so as to elicit the trust of others.

(2) Mastering conflict

Once a thriving family has begun building trust it can draw upon this trust in the face of conflict. If a family feels distrust toward each other it will not be inclined to earnestly address conflict. Trust and trustworthiness lead to goodwill, rapport, and earnest connection. Family members will develop a reserve of goodwill—a deep emotional reserve from which to draw in the face of conflict.

Conflict can be personal or it can be ideological. You engage in personal conflict when you argue about misunderstandings, unmet or competing needs and expectations, and behaviors that cause pain. You engage in ideological conflict when you argue about practices, ideas, issues, beliefs, and principles.

Resolving personal conflict is important to thriving family systems as otherwise a fake harmony creeps into the family culture. Jesus says that we are to take the *initiative* to resolve conflict when others have something against us.[31] Learning to address conflict about ideas can spur the family to rigorously seek and discover new opportunities, understandings, and perspectives. The family can enter into unfiltered, passionate, creative, vigorous debate around issues it believes are important.

Personal conflict can often create great anguish. Families, by the very nature of being a family, face the lifelong challenge of integrating different lives together into one interdependent family. The bumps in the road along the way can temporarily overwhelm, even paralyze your family with fear. Unresolved personal conflict hinders discussion about ideas and values.

If I have not resolved a personal conflict with my wife then I will have difficulty effectively and creatively engaging her in conflict about ideas.

When family members do not trust each other, debate is engaged with the mindset of setting the other straight or of seeking to win at the expense of the other. Or worse, family members betray the other's trust by speak negatively about them or their ideas behind their back. When family members deeply trust one another, they can engage in debate with an open mindset that seeks win-win results—where all benefit.

The table below shows graphically the tension in our choice between two different approaches to handling conflict: harmony and directness. The table shows the benefits of harmony in the upper left box and of directness in the upper right box. The table also shows the draw-backs to both in the lower right and lower left boxes. Every family manages this tension between harmony and directness, sometimes on a case-by-case basis. Ideally, the best place in this table is somewhere close to the top-middle portion. This is the point where the family gets every advantage of engaging in conflict while maintaining constructive harmony.

Conflict

+ Harmony	+ Directness
Constructive, decency is maintained, civility	Passionate, creative, raw conflict, opportunity, differentiation, understanding
Artificial, no conflict, lose-lose –	Destructive, mean-spirited, combative, harmful, win-lose –

Families aren't perfect and don't perfectly engage in conflict. But the power of forgiveness will help your family to recover and build its confidence that it can survive any conflict. Confidence means that when families recover from a big personal conflict they develop closer ties afterward, greater understanding of themselves and their loved one, and a sense of gratitude toward their leader for the stability and strength of their relationship with each other.

Mastering conflict increases our confidence in our relationships, our effectiveness in exploring new ideas, our understanding of ourselves and others, and our ability to capitalize on new opportunities quickly.

(3) Achieving unity

When a family builds trust and masters conflict it has stability for achieving specific commitments together--a unity of purpose. The thriving family's unity of purpose is expressed in its story, including its vision and beliefs. Two aspects of achieving unity are ownership and clarity.

Ownership

When we achieve unity each family member takes ownership or buy-in of what is being committed to. Each family member is earnestly and emotionally invested in the commitment being made.

Unity does not mean uniformity and does not necessarily require unanimity. Unity is not about waiting until every family member agrees. That is unanimity and I believe is a recipe for slow, plodding, frustrating mediocrity. Unanimity is often seen as necessary and valued for any decision involving a group. It conjures up a process of discussion, persuasion, and, perhaps eventually, mutual agreement. Yet, the unity we're talking about is quite different from unanimity, and even from simply going with the majority vote.

The commitment to unity happens exactly when there is *not* agreement on a matter at hand. If there is agreement, then unity is not an issue. However, when there is not agreement a commitment to unity is a way past the short-comings of a voting process. This commitment can occur even in moments of indecision or when no clear "right" answer becomes apparent. Family members can agree to disagree and yet commit to a matter at hand.

One of the members can ask those in the minority if they are willing to commit to what the majority has advocated. If the minority agree to commit, then you have achieved unity and your family's decision in the matter. If not, then continue the tuning-in process.

Key to the commitment process is bringing to bear upon the issue every possible angle, Biblical passage, understanding, fact, opinion, tidbit, resource, study, and experience that might shed light on the matter. If one of your family members facilitates this process of achieving commitment then that person plays an important role in shining every possible ray of light upon the matter at hand.

Prayer is an important habit when seeking to achieve unity. Through prayer, you can seek God's wisdom and the openness to better align with Jesus as you make decisions and cast votes. Bathed in prayer and having gathered information that might shape the decision, a facilitator can muster every ounce of courage and wisdom and propose new solutions when the family is at an impasse. Then, the members decide whether or not they can agree to commit to the proposed idea.

More often than not, members will commit to what the facilitator has chosen. Most folks are reasonable. They do not require that their idea be adopted. They want others to hear their ideas and to acknowledge, understand, and appreciate them as part of the deliberating process toward the final commitment.

While consensus can be profitably used in decision-making, throughout the Bible there are examples of great commitments being achieved after a leader has played a role in bringing forward to the group's attention a particular vision. Paul is given a vision at night of the man from Macedonia calling for Paul to come over and help; he shares the vision with his team and they commit together to act upon the vision.

Clarity

One other factor involved in achieving unity is clarity. Even when family members master the ability to disagree and yet commit to unity, they can still struggle to be effective with their commitment. The reason why is because many families fail to achieve clarity about what they are committing to. Commitments to unity can be ambiguous. When the family is not clear about its commitment it is not in alignment, despite having committed to a matter. The unity can turn ugly as members make well-intended assumptions about what they have agreed to and end up frustrated and confused.

At the end of the gathering to achieve unity one of the members can ask, "*What have we agreed to now?*" This person or someone else writes down what she thinks has been agreed to. All the members can interact with what is written, especially if they remember differently. They then take turns paraphrasing what they understand they have agreed to. The final commitment to unity agreed to is written down by a note-keeper in a dated journal about the gathering.

At family gatherings that follow, different family members can be selected to communicate the commitment made. Knowing that you will be communicating the commitment to unity later on sharpens your sense of ownership in the commitment as it is being made and encourages expressing concerns sooner rather than later.

(4) Embracing mutuality

Once your family has achieved unity it now has a commitment to which each member is mutually supportive of and accountable to. By accountable, I'm not referring to the use of that word as a threat or an announcement of impending punishment, such as, "*Son, I will hold you accountable for your actions!!*" The accountability that I'm referring to is more about a mutual willingness of family members to remind one another when they have not lived up to their commitments. This accountability also applies to situations where the family member appears to be on the verge of missing an agreed upon standard of behavior or performance.

This accountability is most often a direct, one-on-one dynamic. It is based on the idea that when members are accountable to each other they're more motivated to follow through. They do not want to let their loved one(s) down.

Every family member can model the skill of embracing mutuality by lovingly and humbly letting others know when they aren't living by the family principles. Adult members are especially effective when they allow their children to identify their errors. This is a powerful modeling of humility. If the adult members are lax in embracing mutuality and accountability then so likely will the others. If the adult members truly are embracing accountability then the others are more likely to as well.

If you choose not to embrace accountability and to provide constructive feedback then you are letting your family down. You are hurting not only your family, but also each member individually. The Bible says that we are not to think ourselves too important to help others in need but rather to take responsibility for doing the creative best we can with our life.[32] What if you embrace mutuality? What if you step into the discomfort of openly hearing feedback on your behavior? What if you say what needs to be said and address what others need to hear so that they can adapt, learn, and grow?

(5) Focusing on principles

If your family masters the first four skills but does not focus on principles it will be like a hot air balloon being blown whichever way the wind happens to blow. The family of faith tunes in its principles through its relationship with Jesus. The thriving family has highly defined and family-specific faith principles by which it lives.

Let's call these faith principles its *visioning commitments*. Visioning commitments are your own family's unique focus of faith principles that drive your family's existence in relationship with Jesus. Your visioning commitments are tuned in through your relationship with Jesus. These visioning commitments serve the function of guiding, inspiring, encouraging, challenging, and forming the family on its journey with Jesus.

Focusing on principles can also be difficult because there are seemingly zillions of distractions we face daily. One of the biggest threats to focusing on principles is our focus on ourselves. We tend to favor what is comfortable, pleasurable, and desirable for us. But focusing on principles takes us into something larger than ourselves. We may feel discomfort, uncertainty, or anxiety about focusing on principles. But it will take us out of our comfort zone, deeper within ourselves, and further outside ourselves as we take action to serve and build relationships with others. Your family faces the challenge of choosing to put principles ahead of each other and ahead of your family. Then, your family faces the challenge of living out those principles.

When God is the leader of your family, however, your principles take on a whole new level of meaning. You have the ultimate coach, friend, forgiver of souls, and leader for the journey. Your God-guided vision encourages your reliance upon God. Your vision challenges you to follow where God goes, serve where needs are great, and forms you more into the character of Jesus. For families whose leader is God , their vision aligns them in following and moving with God in the unfolding story of God for the world.

What will a thriving family look like that uses these skills? Thriving families develop and balance four aspects of their lives together: faith, growth, mission, and nurture.

Aspects of a thriving family

A thriving family imprints, affirms, lives, and breathes its own story. This cultivates clarity and freedom in its family culture. The essence of the family's story is its vision. This story encourages and guides us to embody and express the character and the unfolding story of God.

Thriving families regularly step back and assess how they're doing as a family in living out their vision. These aspects

—faith, growth, mission, and nurture—are the lens through which a family assesses its journey at any point in time. These aspects are not so much portions of the family's life together as they are aspects of its whole experience as a family. Here is a look at each of the four aspects, the four "*lenses*" through which the thriving family assesses its life together.[33]

The Faith Aspect

While looking through the lens of faith, the thriving family asks itself questions like, "Do we have a growing sense of experiencing:

God: a sense of the holy that transforms, deepens, questions, connects, and enriches?
Community: deep friendship and community with others on our journey?
Discovery: "Aha!" moments—about ourselves and God?
Love: God's unconditional love?
Unity: with creation and compassion for strangers and those different from us?
Joy: gratitude, humility, and celebration?

The Growth Aspect

While looking through the lens of growth, the thriving family asks itself, "Do we experience a growing sense of being:

Knowledgeable: about God, ourselves, and the world?
Resourceful: problem-solving and developing practical life skills?
Intentionally Self-Aware: reflecting and applying?
Whole: a unity between our spiritual, mental, physical, and emotional selves?
Free: engaging in playful experimentation and in questioning and open conversation?
Generous: Donating and sharing what we have been given and are discovering?

The Mission Aspect

While looking through the lens of mission, the thriving family asks itself, "Do we have a growing sense of experiencing:

Urgency: for sharing and embodying the difference God makes for us in our life?
Risk-Taking: playful experimentation in service to others?
Authenticity: that reveals both vulnerability and strength?
Compassion: a heart like Jesus' that donates love and acts justly in a broken world?
Empowered Decision-Making: where we each make decisions for our own mission?
Passion: for transforming the lives of those we serve and build relationships with?

The Nurture Aspect

While looking through the lens of nurture, the thriving family asks itself, "Do we have a growing sense of experiencing:

Unity: support, encouragement, healing and personal transformation with each other?
Balance: time for self-care, playing together, building one-on-one relationships?
Support: given and received in crises and for achieving personal goals?
Community: including family dialogue, conversation, and story-weaving?
Selflessness: committed to the idea that those who seek life must give their life away?
Love: which we donate to, and receive from, each other?

You each are accountable to each other in these essential aspects as expressed in your vision. You will experience a sense of freedom, clarity, and excitement as a thriving family system, whether you are a family of two, three, four or more, with or without children.

Try this self-awareness survey:

If our family did not continue to ______________________ then I would feel sad about our family.

The things that concern me most about our family are ____
____
____.

If our family would ______________________________,
I would feel excited about sharing with others what is happening with our family.

If with a stroke of a pen I could change one thing about our family, I would change ______________________________
____.

Fig. 2

Family Journey Point: Chapter Six

To Ponder: What is Jesus like? What can our family be like? Reflect and share together.

To Consider: Ask God: *Help me and help us become open to expressing and embodying the kind of love that God loves us with.*

To Remember: *"Fix your attention on God. You'll be changed from the inside out. Readily recognize what he wants from you, and quickly respond to it."*

Mark 5:19 (NIV)

Principle #3: Awareness of God

While he was still speaking, a bright cloud enveloped them, and a voice from the cloud said, "This is my Son, whom I love; with him I am well pleased. Listen to him!"

— **Matthew 17:5** (NIV)

Tuning In To God

News about Jesus kept spreading. Large crowds came to listen to him teach and to be healed of their diseases. But Jesus would often go to some place where he could be alone and pray.

Luke 5:15-16 (CEV)

"Can we really tune in to God?"

I was a freshman in college—and loving it. I was also seeking God. I had been experimenting with a habit of praying a prayer that Jesus taught his followers to pray. For a couple of weeks every evening I would pray this prayer. The words of this prayer were the words I would use to pray. By the end of two weeks I began to realize I was ready for more. I needed authenticity and depth. I figured, what other kind of relationship do I have where I say the same thing over and over again and listen quietly in response? It had nothing to do with the prayer and everything to do with me—and God.

Within a week or so, a resident assistant and friend in my dorm, a former football player at the college, approached me, saying, "Hey Skip, would you be interested in coming by my place for a small group time together?" I said, "Sure. What time?" He gave me the time. I showed up. A few other guys were sitting on a couch and chairs around a little coffee table. At the end of one of our times together, he gave me a booklet, ***Seven Minutes with God: How to Plan a Daily Quiet Time*** *and a sheet, "How to Develop a Prayer Plan."*[34] *He spent time, sensitively and non-judgmentally, going over how to pray.*

Your awareness of God, yourself, and your family expands every time you personally encounter God. You are transformed. Your perception and experience of life shift. Encountering God can at the same time be time-stopping, transporting, electric, relieving, and awe-inspiring. You might find yourself in tears, laughing, or both. You might experience a lightness of being, vibrations, goose bumps, or a warm fullness within you. Or you might not. Every person and every family is different. What remains the same, whatever your experience, is that when you accept God's acceptance of you—choosing God to be the leader of your life—the Bible says you receive the gift of God's presence or Spirit within you.[35] In this way, you will have begun the process of tuning in to God.

Tuning in to God is not a one-time event but a life-long process of continually aligning with God. God has taken the first step—loving and accepting you—and when you tune in to God you are taking steps in response.[36] Jesus regularly went off before sunrise by himself for quiet time to pray. Then he would go off to the next town on his mission. *Quiet time fuels active time.* What if you were to continually re-commit to Jesus' leadership of your life and acceptance of Jesus' forgiveness of your soul? Tuning in to God is not like purchasing a life insurance policy that collects dust in your safety deposit box until your family cashes in when you die. It's not like going to the drug store and buying a lifetime supply of aspirin, all at once.

Tuning in to God is all about an ongoing relationship—yours with God. Since you are unique—no one else is quite like you—your relationship with God is unique. You must journey as only you can. In this way, you will be vitally tuning in to God and God's unfolding story for you and for the world. You spend time with those you are close to or want to grow closer with. If you receive the gift of God's presence within you then the process of tuning in to God is a process that includes spending time tuning in to God within you. You make time and space for being with God.

The Bible says that God wants to be your best and most intimate friend.[37] As you open up to God's desire to be your most intimate friend, you will move from being curious about God to being intimate with God. You will move from mostly perceiving God outside of yourself to perceiving God within. You will no longer revere God from a great distance but as an intimate friend and the leader of your life. You will go from talking about God as "*out there*," "*nearby*," or occasionally "*showing up*" to talking about God as within and who nurtures, challenges, teaches, corrects, guides, inspires, and fills you and walks with you on your journey. You will come to sense, know, and experience God as living within you.

Three Ways of Tuning in to God

Three ways by which you can tune in to God are: knowing, experiencing, and participating with God. What if you were to know, experience, and participate with God? You would never be the same again! Your character would, here a little, there a little, become more like that of Jesus.

When you know, experience, and participate with God you allow God to more fully shape you and expand your capacity to live out and express God's unfolding story for the world. You weave a cord of three strands not easily broken—knowing, experiencing, and participating with God.[38]

What do we mean by knowing? Knowing God is a process of getting to know the Master and so expanding your mental awareness of God. What do you understand and think about God? What you think about God sets the trajectory of your spiritual experience. How do you perceive God? What mental pictures do you have? Is God an old, white man with a beard? A maternal natural being known as Mother Nature? Is God an amorphous blob floating around in the air? Does God create and then stand back? Is God a neutral uncaring set of laws of nature that you must adhere to or disregard at your peril? Or is God an infinitely compassionate, emotive, wise, involved, and personal creator?

How you know God is affected by the expectations you have for what God does and who God is. Your perception of God is affected by the words and stories you use, hear, and accept about God.

We had a young children's Bible that said Jesus was a wise and good teacher but nothing about his being the savior. We threw that one out, recycled it, actually.

Another one tells the story of Jesus being baptized in the Jordan River. I was lying down with our children reading it to them. I invited them to pray with me in anticipation of reading the written prayer at the end of the story. I began, "Dear God, help me to . . . ." I paused as I silently caught the words to come. It read, "Dear God, help me to do good things and obey my mom and dad. Amen." I managed to recover from my disappointment and editorially continued on, ". . . help me to learn about, accept, feel, and speak your love, in Jesus' name, amen."

I disliked the words of the written prayer because they had the effect of setting stumbling blocks between the children and God—behaviors that children must perform before they can enjoy connection with God. Later, I grabbed a pen and crossed out, "do good things" with "accept and speak your love."

What songs do you sing, if any, about God? What do you understand about how powerful God is? How loving, compassionate, accepting, forgiving, and wise is God? How attentive is God to you? Does God really know the minute details of your life? Does God care about those details? How much *does* God care about you? These are all questions of perception and how or whether we can perceive God.

What you know about God may change as you experience and participate with God. Most of those who go away on a mission trip do not return the same as they went. They are transformed by their experience. Knowing, experiencing, and participating with God are closely intertwining strands of the process of tuning in to God. For example, let's say you are inspired while standing along the beach, looking out at the vastness, power, and beauty of the ocean, and you experience God. As you do, you will also know God in your mind. If you also were actively listening to a deeply depressed friend share her struggles and God used you to gently and lovingly lead your friend forward in her life then you will have participated with, experienced, and been knowing God all at the same time. You will have been doing what God is doing, hung out with God, and grown in your understanding of God, all at the same time.

Tuning In To God: Knowing God
"Can we know the Master?"
The Bible says that its words are written so that in choosing God as your leader you may *know* God and be part of the forever family of God—not perhaps or maybe, but a certainty of knowing that you are in relationship with God.[39] The Bible says of each of us that we are to "*be transformed by the renewing of your mind*" as a means of tuning in to God and what God wants.[40] The good news is that God will provide for you what you need so that your own messy story can in some way express God's own story for the world.

The journey of knowing the Master—*perceiving God*—invariably has ups and downs, periods of being richly and spiritually nourished and times of feeling spiritually empty, malnourished, and dry. For some, the journey toward knowing the Master arrives at a crisis where they recognize that they alone have chosen not to accept God's love for them, resulting in spiritual dryness, emptiness, and hunger. These folks recognize that they have chosen to separate themselves from

God and harmed themselves and others. Crisis has led them to realize that they have messed up their own lives and are ready to try a different way.

> *One young man in his early 20's left his hometown to go live near the beach. He met another man who introduced him to drugs and heavy alcohol use. The man at various times had hurt his own family and friends even as he was in what he described as "a searching mode." He was looking for acceptance. He felt like he was part of a community with his beach friend.*
>
> *His family prayed for him daily. Growing up, the young man had participated at a church with his family and friends. He admitted, however, "I just wasn't connecting with them."*
>
> *One evening alone in his apartment, broken and despairing, he thought to himself, "I want to go with a better way. This is my last drink of alcohol."*
>
> *"That was my last drink," he recounted. He also sensed that God could somehow use his experience for the benefit of others struggling on their own journey. It was about that time that he was drawn to a church where he now serves on their worship tech support team. He was interviewed about his struggles and the power of God in overcoming them. His interview was broadcast to the congregation one Sunday morning.*[41]

For others, the journey toward knowing the Master takes a different path. While they may recognize that they've made some poor choices along the way, overall, they have managed to raft through the chaos of life without having messed up. They see the young man who chose drugs and alcohol abuse and know he messed up and they have not—not like he has, at any rate. They believe that they've managed through wits, wisdom, guile, beauty, strength, intellect, social skills, whatever they have at their disposal, to keep from messing up and in this way to control their own destiny.

These folks arrive at a crisis when they realize that although they haven't really messed up, neither are they richly nourished. They come to realize that, like the young man who messed up his life, they too are spiritually thirsty and underfed and withered in their soul. They come to realize that their own control of their destiny has led to something like what Thoreau describes as a "*life of quiet desperation.*" They too recognize their need for the nourishment only Jesus can provide. They break their quiet desperation with words like, "*Jesus, help me. I used to think I should win life on my own but now I know better. You say that you knock on the door of my soul. I'm opening the door—please come in!*"

Because the Master Jesus was and is perfect, he was and is in perfect union with God and God with him.[42] Therefore, any perception of God will include, conscious or not, a perception of Jesus. You cannot divorce Jesus from your process of perceiving God without contradicting yourself.[43] Trying to journey toward God and perceive God without ultimately acknowledging or relating with Jesus is contradictory, like trying to hold your loved one's hand but not wanting to touch them. It isn't going to happen. You can pretend to hold their hand and ignore the truth or you can hold their hand and embrace them and be embraced. Whichever way your journey has gone, the process of perceiving God ultimately must be led by the leader of your family—God. Know this: *You can know the Master!*

The Bible

The principal way to know the Master and perceive God in depth is through the Bible. The Bible is the inspired God-breathed history and words of the movement and story of God. The Bible provides awareness about who you are, who God is, your need for God, what God does to restore you to community with God and other human beings, and how you can tune in to God and be part of God's unfolding story for the world.[44]

The Bible says that God sent forth God's word into the world and the word was the person of Jesus.[45] God interrupted human history in the birth, life, death, and resurrection of Jesus. When you open the Bible, you are opening, in effect, a written avenue to Jesus, who is the live version of what is written. In encountering the written words you can encounter Jesus.

While God cannot be contained within the written words, stories, and pages of the Bible—because God is larger than words—God inspires the words and infuses the words with power and meaning. God uses the images of the words on the page as a means for accomplishing God's vision—inviting all into the forever family of God, teaming with God in God's movement for the world.

Every time you engage with the words and the God whom they point to you can discover new understanding, insight, and guidance. The words of the Bible are like a multi-faceted gem which yields new light with every turn. The stories of the Bible become your stories as you engage with God in them. You experience your creation in the creation story, your freedom and discovery in the story of the Israelites being freed from slavery in Egypt and wandering the desert. You are not so much reading and studying as encountering Jesus as the *Living Word*.

While the Bible is the principal means for revealing and pointing to God and is itself the story of God for the world, you can at some level perceive God in many different ways. Everyone is different, including in their spiritual temperament or way of getting to know the Master and perceiving God. Some are more intellectual, others more mystical, some benefit more from a traditional approach, others thrive in getting outdoors, and so on. Realize that you may want to tailor how you get to know God with your own spiritual temperament.[46]

Tuning In To God: Experiencing God
"Can we hang out with the Master?"

If knowing the Master, perceiving God, is about being mentally aware of God then hanging out with the Master—*experiencing God*—is about the *depth* of our awareness of God.

What do we mean by experiencing? Experiencing God is a process of encountering the Master and so expanding your total awareness of God to the point where you trust the reality of God more even than you trust that the sun will rise in the morning. You expand your awareness of God in such a way that is more vibrantly real than your awareness of your spouse or best friend. You give God pleasure when you trust and adore God with your whole being down to the core of your soul. When you surrender to and worship God in such a way that you not only embrace the Master with all your mind, heart, and strength, but also with your soul, then God smiles and you are hanging out with the Master and experiencing God.[47]

How can I get my mind, heart, body, and soul tuned in to God?

As you surrender to God as the leader of your life and your family, you will discover that God both dwells within you and is around you. You will not want to miss experiencing God within yourself nor with others who are on the journey.

> *I was sensing a call to serve as a pastor. Yet, I knew all too well my own weaknesses. I had hearing loss from the measles when I was four and had developed Type I Diabetes. The summer before I began seminary, I worked at a large national bank in the San Francisco Bay Area as a temporary employee. On a break in the lobby of the*

bank I asked God, "Is going to seminary a good decision for me? I mean, you and I know my strengths but also my weaknesses, you better than I." This was weighing on me. So I went off outside and began to walk around the block. "Do I go or do I not go?" I pondered.

I came upon a series of small shops. The sign of one caught my eye. "This Is the Place," it said. I chuckled. Walked in. A stationery store. I was immediately drawn to one greeting card on the shelf straight in front of me as I walked in, even before I could see its message. I didn't look at any other cards in the store. I stepped up to the card and picked it up. The front of the card had a picture of Jesus with a shepherd's staff in his hand with a pastoral landscape and sheep around him.

The card had Jesus saying, "I never said it would be easy." Now, this was a cheesy five-and-dime card. I mean, the Jesus on the card looked northern European rather than Mediterranean and wore colorful robes that he likely never wore. But the message was his to me. My heart seemed to stop. I sighed and then chuckled. My body and soul felt inundated with his presence. I walked back out onto the streets, around the block, and into the bank.

When seeking specific guidance, be sure to ask God for wisdom for making a wise decision. Because you are unique, the journey of getting your body, mind, and soul tuned in to and aligned with God will have its own unique character. There is no one-size-fits-all, quick-fix formula for experiencing God. Hanging out with God, like growing in your knowledge and understanding of God, is all about an ongoing relationship and journey with God. You can experience God while running a copy machine at work, standing in line at the Department of Motor Vehicles, sitting in your car in rush-hour traffic, while shopping at the grocery store, and while being still in prayer. You will awaken this way of experiencing and being aware of

God through prayer and adoration of God.

You will come to know both God and yourself through this journey of prayer. You will come to know that you are a piece or a portion of God, experience this reality, and participate with God in God's unfolding story for the world. Understand that you are not God but you have within you god-ness–that which is the image of God. The Bible says that God created you and knew you as a spiritual being before your existence on Earth.[48] Most significantly, you will experience God abiding within you. Jesus says, "*abide in me, and I will abide in you.*"[49] Understanding and exploring this reality will mark a major shift in your awareness of your self, God within you, and the world you live in.

Learn from Jesus who regularly prays in solitude and realize that prayer is essential to experiencing God. Prayer at heart is seeking out, being filled with, and being aware of God. Prayer can include listening to, speaking with, and experiencing God. While there are many types of prayer—one writer counts over fifty—below are a few that I think may be especially helpful to explore and try on for size. If you already have different prayer methods that you like, stay with them and cultivate a growing experience of God dwelling within you.

Note to parents with young children: Pray with your children daily, perhaps at bedtime, before they leave for school, and spontaneously as you or your children are moved to. One parent described how he prays with each child as they head off for school, praying for their protection. You could also pray thanks to God for your child's opportunity to learn, make new friends, and share their own ideas throughout the day or that your child be open to God teaching them throughout the day.

Spoken Prayer

This is the most common, widely accepted, and used form of prayer. Verbal prayer is using words, spoken aloud or silently, in talking with God. Many of the Psalms in the middle of the Bible are a good example. Spoken prayer can involve listening as much as speaking. One pastor prayed, "*Lord, how much should I be asking you for the church's general budget each month?*" Then he listened. "*Two thousand dollars a month*," came the reply.[50] While we can, like this pastor, receive specific guidance, it is not necessary nor does the Bible represent that it should be sought or expected for being faithful in following God. I expect that had the pastor prayed, "*Lord, give me wisdom for making a wise decision that honors you and your church*," he would have arrived at the same answer.

Some folks feel inhibited about or wary of prayer. They might feel a lack of integrity about prayer because they don't know God. Or they feel hesitant to pray because they aren't sure God exists and would feel foolish about praying to a god that doesn't exist. They might feel wary about prayer because the idea of talking and listening to God seems heavy to them, intimidating, or requires a commitment they don't want to make. Some folks have had bad experiences where a leader uses prayer to make a speech or to sermonize and appear self-important in his prayer. Others have prayed extensively but feel as though God hasn't heard their prayers or responded in a way they hadn't expected or wanted.

Have you ever noticed that when a person talks about someone else you can learn more about them than the person they're talking about? You can learn a lot about someone by listening to them pray! Having said that, understand that your prayer is between you and God. There are no prayer police to accost you for praying in a wrong or unacceptable way. Use words that you'd use in talking with a friend at your kitchen table. Address God however you are comfortable. If you like, you can begin, "*Dear God, . . .*" and continue from there. You can end your prayer with, "*amen*," or "*in Jesus' name, amen*." Be honest with God. God knows even better than you your desires, troubles, and heart.

If God already knows what's on my heart and in my mind, why pray? Isn't that silly? God wants you to personally engage with God on the journey. Jesus regularly says, "*Come, follow me … Come and see.*"[51] He says, "*What do you want me to do for you?*"[52] God has feelings, can feel and express compassion, empathy, joy, harsh truth, pain, hurt, and love. By acknowledging and expressing your internal life with God you will accept and open up a rapport with God who will work in your life. God's presence within you will come alive. And you will experience God.

As you become more intimate with God, you will experience God as you verbally pray. You might feel a tingling sensation in your head or throughout your body or you might not. You might feel a lightness, as though you are being gently lifted up or not. You might feel a resonant energy within you or not. Whatever the case, you can experience God. Prayer with words can be especially powerful when including words, phrases, or verses from the Bible. You will also experience God in the results that take place in your life as a result of your verbal prayer time with God.

> *My wife and I were searching for a house close by to the church I was pastor to in southern California. We initially had bought a house in a city further east. Housing was expensive. We had been searching for months without success. One afternoon, we put an offer above the listing price on what we thought was a spectacular condominium and thought our offer would be accepted. Someone else walked in later that afternoon and paid cash for the full amount.*
>
> *I explored this with God in prayer. I was studying Psalm 15 at the time. I decided to memorize the first verse—O Lord, who may abide in your tent? Who may dwell on your holy hill?—and apply it to our house search. We realized that our search wasn't about finding the "perfect" house but*

about dwelling with God in the midst of the search. Every time I felt tempted to seek the perfect home, I committed to resisting that thought by praying and quoting aloud Psalm 15:1.

After making that commitment, we looked at a couple of different condominiums. I included Psalm 15:1 in prayer while at each place. Our offer on a less spectacular but nice condo was quickly accepted and we were grateful.

Awareness Prayer

This can be a powerful prayer for becoming aware of the presence of God and more present with the other members of your family.[53] This prayer invites us to identify moments at the end of a meeting, event, day or week, where we felt most open and connected toward God's presence and love and when we were most closed, forgetful, or disconnected. This prayer involves prayerfully asking and answering two questions:

For what moment am I most grateful?
For what moment am I least grateful?

Other possible questions to ask are:

In what moment was I most loving?
In what moment was I least able to love?

In what moment did my family seem most alive?
In what moment did my family seem least alive?

When did my family feel most free?
When did my family feel least free?

When did my family give and receive the most love?
When did my family give and receive the least love?

Prayerfully posing these pairs of questions clears the way for identifying your moments of connection and disconnect with God, yourself, and others. As you pay attention to these two types of moments in your life you become more aware of how God can be present in your day and life. Occasionally you will see a pattern of being aligned with God's love and movement for the world. Other times you will see how you are in some way blinded or absorbed in your own wounds or difficulty. Let me suggest a process for this prayer.

Find a place to pray without interruption. Light a candle, set out an open Bible, or otherwise create a set-aside space that reminds you of God's presence within you. Spend a few moments in silence, becoming more aware of God's presence, power, and nurture of you.

Ask the Master to be within you and to lead you as you explore your latest family encounter. It might be a family gathering, event, meal together, or an informal interaction with family.

Ask, "For what moment am I most grateful?" As you play back in your mind's eye the event or interaction, allow small exchanges, seemingly little objects or interactions to emerge—a touch, a gesture, smile, laugh, kind word, greeting, a conversation, or a smile—in which you were most grateful. Stay with whatever moment God seems to provide for you. Be open and let this moment come forward in your mind's eye.

Let all else fade away as you spend a few moments turning the gem of this moment of gratitude. In this moment, what did you experience? What were you like? What was your family like? What might God be seeking to teach you through this experience? Write down or journal any insights that come to you. Share these insights with Jesus and see what develops.

Ask, "For what moment am I least grateful?" Review in your mind's eye your experience with your family. Allow God to draw to your attention whatever moment in which you seemed somehow blocked from the flow of God's love and presence. Write down or journal any insights. Share these insights with Jesus and see what happens.

Breath Prayer

This form of prayer powerfully embodies you in your prayer and can be a powerful, yet simple, way of experiencing God. Here's how it works. Select a Biblical phrase, like *I am a child of God*. Break the phrase into two parts, a first part and a second part. For the first part, you breathe in through your nose, hold your breath for four seconds or so, then for the second part, breath out through your mouth.

For the phrase *I am a child of God,* slowly and steadily breathe in through your nose while silently speaking the word *I am*. Hold your breath for four or five seconds then you slowly and in a controlled fashion breathe out through your mouth while silently speaking the words *a child of God*. Repeat this pattern of prayer as often as you want. You can use whatever phrase you wish. The Bible provides many other phrases to choose from as well.

Centering Prayer

This form of prayer cultivates awareness and alignment with God, both in the prayer time itself and afterward. The goal of this prayer is not to have fabulous experiences of God, though you may likely have them, but to be about the practice of intentionally letting go and surrendering to God. In this prayer you will begin with the intention of being totally available and open to God. You will give yourself utterly to God. You will let go of any thought that comes to mind. You may want to begin this centering prayer time with an introductory phrase or prayer, such as saying aloud, "*Be still and know that I am God.*"

Here's the deal: if you catch yourself thinking, let the thought go. Whenever a thought comes to mind, silently speak a special word you have chosen in advance to let go of the thought and return to open availability with God. Your word could be: God, Spirit, peace, love, open, filled, still, deep, yes, shalom, Jesus, receive, agape (Greek for love), Adonai (Hebrew for Lord), river, etc. It's not so much the word you choose as it is simply choosing one that will accomplish the task of returning you to openness with God. Keep in mind that you will likely have to use your word to ease away from thoughts and into a higher awareness of God and self many times as you get started.[54] Imagine and become aware of the presence of God within you. Here's the process:

- **Commit to spending twenty minutes in centering prayer;**
- **Be clear and strong in your intention of becoming available and open to God;**
- **Do the "deal": if you catch yourself thinking, let your thought go;**
- **Use your special word as many times as necessary to let go of thought and return to being open and available with God.**

In addition, this prayer is a powerful way to experience change in your life. By applying what you experience and do in this prayer to the stresses of your daily life, you can dramatically transform the way you respond in stressful situations.

Applying centering prayer

The goal of applying centering prayer to our lives is to cultivate a perspective that is in alignment with God in the midst of stress–that's a powerful combination! Physically, we will experience making ourselves open and willingly vulnerable in the face of stress or difficulty.

Imagine that you are having a big fight with your spouse or friend, or that you have a big disagreement with your boss, or your child is missing. What happens physically? Is your gut tightening? Are you bracing yourself, drawing inwardly? Is your breathing shallow? Are you moving into a circle-the-wagons defensive posture? The application of centering prayer involves making your centering prayer an experience of being open to God a reference point in moments of stress. Here are three R's for applying centering prayer and intentionally aligning with God in the midst of stress:

- **Recognize your gut tightening**, bracing yourself, clenching, shallow breathing, and so on.

- **Recall your experience in centering prayer** earlier in the day, including how you felt physically: free, released, open, vulnerable, receptive, aligned with the power and love of God.

- **Release your tightness**, clenching, and being bound up in the moment of stress. Choose to let go and align your body with God and its relaxed state during your centering prayer experience.

As you deepen your connection with God, you may experience feelings of grief and sorrow. Through prayer you will journey not only in movement with God for the world but also within yourself, exploring dormant feelings, hurts, pain, and suffering. You will also become more compassionate and empathic for the suffering of the world. You will be empowered to do this because the power within you—God's presence—is greater than any power outside of you in the world. You will more and more be able to hold in tension the suffering of the world with a joy surpassing all human understanding.

Tuning In To God: Participating With God
"Can we do what the Master does?"

If hanging out with God is a quality of the depth of our awareness of God then doing what the Master does –*participating with God*–is the exclamation point of our awareness of God while on the planet.

What do we mean by participating with God? We go from being spectators to players, from being cheerleaders–which, by the way, is a productive role–to proactive partners in God's unfolding story for the world. We become part of God's team in what God is doing among all people. We behave in such a way that aligns with the mysterious movement of God. As we resonate with our leader, our character and our actions become more like those of our leader.

This third strand of the cord of spiritual growth is not dependent upon the other two strands. You can start participating with God as soon as you can say, "*Yes*" to an opportunity. However, you will be more effective for God as you weave the other two strands with this one, habitually cultivating renewal in what you know about God and making time to hang out with God.

The Bible tells us to not merely listen to, or perceive, the word but do what it says.[55] Do what you are inspired to do as you perceive and experience God. Nothing is more essential than fulfilling the purpose of your soul and spirit's existence. Participating with God, then, can be exciting, vital, and adventurous. It can also be drudgery, dangerous, and painful. You will likely encounter and experience suffering and grief.

Taking action can energize, deepen, and profoundly transform your journey. There's nothing like stepping out and serving in a way that has ultimate significance. There are an infinite number of ways that you can participate with God, whether structured or spontaneous. The best way to get started is to step in and get your feet wet. Try it on for size. You might later discover that you are better suited for a different role but don't let that discourage you. Instead, let this discovery move you forward ever more fully, ever more aware of God.

Family Journey Point: Chapter Seven

To Ponder: What would it be like to listen to God? What do you suppose you would hear? Share together your thoughts.

To Consider: What if you were to spend time being refueled in hanging out with God and time going out and living and telling God's story for the world?

To Remember: *"Jesus would often go to some place where he could be alone and pray"*

Luke 5:16 (CEV)

The Characteristics of a Follower

8

And so we are transfigured much like the Messiah, our lives gradually becoming brighter and more beautiful as God enters our lives and we become like him.

2 Corinthians 3:18b (MSG)

"Am I the hands, heart, and voice of God?!"

Janet, John, and their two daughters, aged 7 and 8, after having lunch with a homeless family invited the family to come live with them. The family consisted of a woman, Nola, a man, Josh, and their two year-old boy, Andrew. Nola was six months pregnant. They were living in a tiny camper trailer hooked to their ragged van parked down the street in a vacant lot.

Janet and John set them up in the family room area in the basement of their 1,600 square-foot house. The room included a hide-a-bed for them to sleep on. Josh was a carpenter who looked for odd jobs. Nola, a college graduate, provided care for Andrew. Janet and John knew that Josh and Nola were struggling and had their own personal issues. They kept praying, "God, we want to do what you want for us and for Josh, Nola, and Andrew. Let the shield of your protecting love surround our girls as we partner with you...."[56]

A follower of Jesus lives to the beat of a different drummer than society and yet lives confidently and humbly in the midst of the woes and brokenness around her. She has an uncanny knack for building rapport and relationships with others, no matter their background, struggles, or successes. Suffering, brokenness, and bad behavior do not cause her to shy away.

Seeing and knowing those suffering from alcoholism, depression, drug abuse, domestic violence, those trapped with heavy debt and mortgages, those who live with lies, denial, lust, and greed, the follower of Jesus engages rather than disengages. He lives in the midst of a paradox of being both one who is broken and prone to mistakes and one made whole in accepting that Jesus accepts him and is the leader of his life.

As a result, she identifies simultaneously with the woeful brokenness around her as well as with the wholeness she is gifted with in her relationship with Jesus. She expresses empathy and understanding. Success as the world measures success does not impress her. She emphasizes accepting others, relationships, and communication in everything he does. She uses the way she is shaped to embody something of the message and presence of God.

Doesn't it seem presumptuous, though, to be hands like those of Moses who parted the Red Sea? Or a voice like that of Peter's speaking transformative news to thousands? Or a heart like that of Andrew's inviting his brother Peter and others to come and see the Master?

Even more presumptuous, that your hands are like those who healed a blind man by forming mud with dirt and spit and spreading it on the blind man's eyes? Or, that your hands are like those that took up the weight of the world's mistakes when nails hung them upon a cross? Or, that your voice is like that which commanded calm upon the stormy sea? Or, that your heart is like the one that had compassion upon even the worst of the world? Can you be the hands, heart, and voice of God?

Clearly, your hands, heart, and voice are not Jesus' hands, heart, and voice. You are not Jesus. Yet, because of who Jesus is and what he does for you, you can keep on becoming more like him. You can become one with him. As such, his hands become your hands, his heart becomes your heart, and his voice becomes yours. You are a separate individual, yet one with him. You are free to choose your own way, yet you choose to follow the way of Jesus.

Every follower is unique and is shaped differently for different ways of serving. However, Jesus' followers share some common characteristics. **One of them is is that their character becomes more like Jesus' as they journey with him.** As a follower of Jesus, you will become more aware of how God is at work within you, and in this way become more aware of God.

The Characteristics of a Follower:

Following Jesus

Followers of Jesus are in the practice of seeking out, relying on, and learning from Jesus. The reference point for everything they do is Jesus himself. The Bible describes Jesus as being alive today and one with God; followers do as Jesus did and follow God, becoming one with God through Jesus.[57] They follow Jesus by worshiping him, spending time supporting and encouraging one another, growing in understanding about Jesus, God, and themselves, spending uninterrupted time hanging out with him, and doing what he is doing for the world.

Quiet time fuels action time

Followers of Jesus balance their time between quiet time hanging out with Jesus and going out and doing what he is doing for the world. Quiet time fuels action time. You have an unlimited resource you can tap into for going back out for the world. If you run out of energy or love for serving others and for expressing compassion for others, you are reminded, much like a gas gauge needle entering the red zone, to stop and refuel. Stop speaking, moving, acting, rushing, running around, and worrying. Refuel in stillness with God, drinking from the infinite reservoir you have access to when you hang out with God.

While sometimes you experience spiritual, emotional, physical, or mental drought and at other times bounty, you know the well from which you draw. You know the source of the love you are called to express. You know that you need balance between doing and being.

If you spend too much time being still, your opportunities to embody and express God's story for the world narrow. If you spend too much time being active, you become disconnected from God in what you do. You begin to behave as though you *should* do what you are doing rather than as though you are aligned with a personal and infinite love that flows through you.

Spontaneous

Followers make themselves available to be used at any time. Jesus encountered folks who would step between him and where he was going. Yet, they were not interruptions on his journey but rather were moments of encounter and opportunities for expressing God's way.

As a follower, you are not so much interrupted from your own important tasks as presented with meaningful moments to engage with others. You do not so much have accidents occur in your life as you have meaningful moments to be awake and engage with. Your journey is truly a journey. There are no accidents that derail your journey, or even pit stops that delay your journey. Instead, your journey includes everything and everyone you encounter and engage with, and more.

Humorous

Followers express and use humor often. The ultimate joke is God's in overcoming the sting of death raising Jesus from the dead. As a follower, nothing can overpower your soul and spirit, not even death itself. Therefore, you have reason to be light-hearted and to breathe new perspective and light into any circumstance along your journey. Your use of humor reminds others not to take themselves or their situation too seriously. Humor helps you claim that you have, after all, a sure hope of life no matter the circumstance.

Compassionate

Followers have a heart for those who are suffering. Followers feel for others in their pain, sorrow, grief, confusion, and despair, as well as in their joy, laughter, giddiness, and gladness. Followers are able to be self-less in their experience of life. They can quiet their own inner life so they can be present with others in theirs. There are times when followers will speak their own feelings, thoughts, and experiences as a way of engaging with others. But there are also times when they will quiet their own inner life to empathize with the inner life of others.

As a follower, you feel sorrow and pain when a friend is dying of cancer. You feel joy when a youth is ecstatic at being accepted into college or into the armed forces. You feel gladness when another is celebrating marriage. You feel for others easily and effusively.[58]

Passionate

Followers are passionate about being with God, enjoying God, and doing what God is doing. You are passionate about becoming all that God put you on the planet to be, becoming daily more like your leader Jesus.

A friend of mine, a successful mortgage executive, struggled with the upheaval around him as banks and mortgage companies closed. He reflected with me on how to better integrate his faith and spirituality into his work. He had caught himself saying, "I work my tail off, getting to work early, sometimes leaving late. I come home to my wife and children and engage my spiritual life."

Your spirituality oozes out of every pore of your being and every activity you take on, whether work, family, hobbies, chores, or rest. It bathes and shapes your thoughts, work, relationships, conversations, and even your breathing.

Creator and Donator of Love

Those who follow Jesus look to cultivate love in their families, homes, work, relationships with others, and with all whom they meet. They continually examine their behavior to see whether they are expressing love. You, as a follower, claim God's unconditional love—a love with no strings attached—for you and for your family. You are seeking behaviors that express, create, and donate the kind of love that God expresses, creates, and donates.

You, having access to this love, have an unlimited supply of this love. Streams of this love flow through you. You actively give this love away, indiscriminately. You surprise others with unexpected, unprompted expressions of unconditional love. You behave as a conduit or a channel of acceptance and love.

Leading like Jesus

Followers know that God has plans bigger than they can imagine or fully grasp. They know that they are called both to be followers and leaders in participating with God in God's plans for the world. Followers seek to make the most of what they've been given and to live out their lives for God's purpose and vision for them. They understand that God intends for them to take a role in and use their influence to embody and express God's unfolding story for the world—*as leaders*!

Jesus calls apprentices those whom he nurtures as both followers and leaders. He builds relationships with others in such a way as to nurture their own leadership qualities. He kneels down before his apprentices and washes their feet, saying, "*This is how I want you to lead—by being in a posture of serving others.*" As a follower, Jesus provides you with a guiding vision for your life as a leader. It also happens that he has already provided for victory—he has defeated evil in his own death and resurrection. The task now is to become like him and to journey with as many as possible as they claim the victory for themselves and for all. He provides a lot of room for your tasks as a leader. He provides himself as an ultimate and constant resource in your role as leader. He sets out the vision and then gives you the freedom to use your own unique gifts to be a leader and accomplish what no one thought possible.

Living their Vision

Jesus gives followers a vision of going out and walking alongside others--a vision of inviting them to follow Jesus, learn from him, know him, hang out with him, and do what he does for the world. As a follower, you embody this vision and journey with others one step at a time, always connected with God in God's unfolding story for the world.

As the leader of your family, God also partners with you in tuning in a unique vision for you and your family within this larger vision for all of God's family. Your unique vision fits your family's shapes, experiences, background, and journey. This vision fits like a glove with your relationship with Jesus. It is the heartbeat of your family's existence.

Your vision orients and motivates your family as it daily journeys with Jesus. While you can use words to describe the vision you tune in, the words don't wholly describe the phenomenon that is this vision. Your vision is more a heartbeat than a document, more an energy-field than a slogan, more a mindset and calling than a series of tasks. Your vision reminds you of who you are and whose you are. It inspires a holy melody of music, so to speak, that is your relationship with your leader Jesus, who fills you with his own mind and heart for the world.

Family Journey Point: Chapter Eight

To Ponder: What would it be like to listen to God? What do you suppose you would hear? Share together your thoughts.

To Consider: What if you were to spend time being refueled in hanging out with God and time going out and living and telling God's story for the world?

To Remember: *"Our lives become brighter and more beautiful as God enters our lives"*

2 Corinthians 3:18b (MSG)

Principle #4: Vision

Then afterward I will pour out my spirit on all flesh; your sons and your daughters shall prophesy, your old men shall dream dreams, and your young men shall see visions. Even on the male and female slaves, in those days, I will pour out my spirit.

— **Joel 2:28-29** (NRSV)

The Power of a Vision

The Jewish believers who came with Peter were amazed that the gift of the Holy Spirit had been poured out on the Gentiles, too.

Acts 10:44-45 (NIV)

"What can we expect will happen?"

James was not a follower of Jesus. He had been married fourteen years and lived in the mid-west. He was a high-level manager with a regional building materials supplier, earning a very high salary with many perks and benefits easily totaling six figures. A year after divorcing, he chose to follow Jesus. He felt drawn to developing ways to relieve human suffering and transform people's lives. Two years later, he married Donna. Donna had a passion for missions overseas and a masters degree in educational counseling. She worked at a local Christian school as a guidance counselor.

After raising and seeing off James' four children to college, they left their careers, and sold the large beautiful home they had built and most of their possessions. This financed his going back to school at Multnomah Bible College in Portland, Oregon, for a bachelors degree in bible and inter-cultural studies.

While in Portland, James worked part-time as an executive pastor with a nearby church whose passion was planting new churches. After graduating at age 47, they sold their Portland home and all their remaining possessions, packed the rest of their belongings into ten suitcases and boxes and headed to Kosovo.

They have now been in Kosovo two years. During the first year James and Donna spent full time learning Albanian.

He is now the director at a center where their outreach and ministry includes a coffee shop, bookstore, copy store, and internet cafe. They provide low-cost ESL and computer classes to the locals. They have an occupational therapist and dream of offering business classes, seminars, and starting small businesses to help provide jobs in an economy with unemployment at around 40 to 50%. Over half the population there is 24 and under. Donna hopes to use her skills as a professional counselor and to mentor and raise up a generation of Kosovar Christian women leaders. Along with the rest of their team, they are seeing Kosovars come to faith in Jesus along with helping to plant missional churches in a very unreached corner of the world.[59]

A family vision impacts not just your family and your relationship with God as your leader but also your neighbors, extended family, friends, co-workers, and all whom you come in contact with. Your family vision changes your family dynamics, outlook, experiences, and perspective through time. Your vision provides an environment for your family to develop its leadership skills.

Your family vision has no power in and of itself. Your vision only has power and impact as it continually points you back to your relationship with Jesus. Your vision orients and motivates your family as it daily journeys with Jesus. Your vision goes hand-in-hand with God's leadership of your family, filling you with the same mind and heart for the world that is in Jesus. *That is power.*

The news of God's unconditional acceptance through Jesus quickly jumped from impacting hundreds of Jewish people in Palestine to thousands and then toward humanity as a whole as the vision spread of God's intent for the destiny of the world. *That is power.*

Yet the power of your relationship with Jesus, and by extension, your vision, is different from the world of competition. The Bible says that our strength comes from weakness and not from any inherent power of our own.[60] The power of your vision, then, is its inspiration, reminder, and focus for you to behave as Jesus behaves, serving others gently, humbly, with perfect love, and abundantly. Like the power of Jesus sitting on a lowly donkey as he rode into Jerusalem on his way to the cross, this power serves the unfolding story of God for all humanity. Your vision turns upside down the assumptions and ways of the world.

Your vision, besides creating excitement, provides you with a practical framework for putting your faith into action. This happens when your family comes into agreement with each other and alignment with God about its vision. Your family may have to come into this alignment in the face of different opinions, choices, and temptations. But you have a sustained, consistent, principled focus as you raft through the chaotic waters of life. Your vision provides the basis for making wise decisions.

Your vision itself is enormous. The accomplishment of your vision is impossible without Jesus as your leader. The challenge of your vision spurs your family onward in a journey partnering with God for the world. Your awareness, vision, compassion, empathy, and thoughts expand. Whereas before you lived in a house, now you live in a neighborhood. Before you knew the names of your neighbors; now you know their struggles. Before you lived for yourselves; now you live for others. Before you knew the folks of the church you attend; now you know people of other faiths and of no faith. Before you hung out with familiar people; now you spend time getting to know unfamiliar people!

The idea of partnering with God itself is enormous. Many think partnering with God is not realistic. Some believe that saying that you have such a partnership does not respect the *otherness* and power of God. This line of thinking says, "Who are we that we would coordinate with God, let alone partner with God, on a project of eternal importance? We are the creatures and God is the creator. God is in control and will take care of the big picture. Our role is to be thankful, not partners." My purpose here is not to belittle my friends who take this position. I honor and support their earnest desire to be faithful, but I disagree.

Why does partnering with God make sense? The Bible consistently states that our posture toward God in light of what God does for us should be gratitude. We are reasonably and rightfully grateful when we accept what God does for us. Being ever grateful, we are highly motivated to actively participate with God.

The second reason partnering with God makes sense is that God directly commissions us to partner with God in telling and living God's unfolding story for the world.[61] Jesus says that we are to go and accomplish God's purpose: to share the news of God's gift through Jesus of being part of God's forever family. We receive God's commission and respond with obedience, again, motivated by gratitude.

The third reason partnering with God makes sense is that if we are in communion with God then we are one with God—who is actively bringing about God's realm—and all God has created. Through the gift of God represented by the bread and cup that we share together in the Jesus meal we come into communion with God. Being gifted with communion with God, we are therefore also in partnership with God through that same gift.

The fourth reason partnering with God makes sense is that the Bible tells us God wants to develop in us the character of Jesus.[62] Being shaped more into the image of God and the character of Jesus means that, over time, we behave more like Jesus, who perfectly participates with God.

The power of your vision increases when you choose to tune in your vision with God as your leader. Your vision is inspired by your family's leader. The character, words, and presence of Jesus, together with the written Bible as a whole, provide guidance for tuning in your vision and so empowering your vision.

The power of your vision is enhanced because you tune in your vision with a growing awareness of your self and your family. You can be honest about your own shortcomings because you are no longer overwhelmed by them. Instead, the power within you is now greater than the power outside of you. You have newfound courage. You no longer need to be defensive about who you are and are not. For the first time, you can be utterly and freely honest, knowing that you are no longer doomed to rely upon pulling yourself up by your bootstraps.

You grow in your awareness of your own weaknesses, your own tendency to make mistakes, and those of your family. You are aware of the whispers that you and your loved one inherit from your families of origin. You are also aware of your family's own giftedness for expressing God's way in your relationships with others. You travel a unique journey and can uniquely partner with God for the world.

The power of your vision is multiplied because you tune in your vision with a growing awareness of God. Your relationship with God continues to grow. You grow in your ability to know God and to be knowledgeable about God. You grow in intimacy with God as you hang out with God. You become more aware of God as you participate with God. As a result, the power of your vision is greater.

When you have a focused vision you have a specific aim and purpose. Without a vision you wander aimlessly. You become defined by your messy family story and the messy world you live in. With a vision, you can more easily tune in to what God wants and make wise decisions in all you face as a family. Your vision makes clear what you are on the planet for and what you are not on the planet for. By having a vision, you journey with a constant awareness of your relationship with God and your God-given task of being a testimony to the news of God's gift of perfect unconditional love.[63]

Your vision creates an open space for being creative and wise in making decisions that honor God. Your family is inspired by your vision, which is an extension of your relationship with Jesus. Being clear about your vision and about a baseline of unacceptable behaviors creates a large creative space between the two in which your family can thrive.

> *In one episode of the reality television show Super Nanny, controlling parents of young children find the courage to go on a vacation in their camper. With Super Nanny's coaching and encouragement, the parents, together with the children, set up red flags around the camp site at a distance beyond which the parents do not want the children to go (and where they cannot see them). With all the flags set up, Super Nanny turns to the camera and with a sly smile says, "Now they have room to play."*[64]

Your family's vision creates a large area of freedom within which your family can journey and make decisions, based on clear parameters.

Your vision cultivates an environment in which healthy conflict can occur. Ambiguity creates stress, uncertainty, subjective and unspoken agendas, ego-driven desires, and an unstable environment in which to make decisions and to engage with each other about our conflicts and differences. Your vision, on the other hand, creates an environment of spoken, and written agreement about the essentials of who you are as a family. You each have a foundation from which you can engage directly, confidently, humbly, and bathed in abundant forgiveness for yourself and for your loved ones.

Your vision has power the moment you make a commitment to it, even though you have barely begun. There is great power in the commitment itself.

> *A Scottish expedition to the Himalayas shared its inspiration in their commitment to the process of planning and accomplishing the climbing of great peaks. They talked about what happens when people commit together:*
>
> *"Until one is committed there is hesitancy, the chance to draw back, always ineffectiveness. Concerning all acts of initiative and creation, there is one elementary truth, the ignorance of which kills countless ideas and splendid plans: that the moment one definitely commits oneself, then Providence moves too. All sorts of things occur to help one that would never otherwise have occurred. A whole stream of events issues from the decision, raising in one's favor all manner of unforeseen incidents and meetings and material assistance, which no one could have dreamt would have come his/her way."*[65]

The power of your vision is in the journey. You commit to live for the world as with the same heart and mind as your leader, who says, "*I'll be with you as you go.*"[66]

Family Journey Point: Chapter Nine

To Ponder: How can we receive God's power within us? Share your thoughts.

To Consider: What if you were to have the same mind and heart for the world that is in Jesus?

To Remember: *"But the Holy Spirit will come upon you and give you power. Then you will tell everyone about me...everywhere in the world."*

Acts 1:8 (CEV)

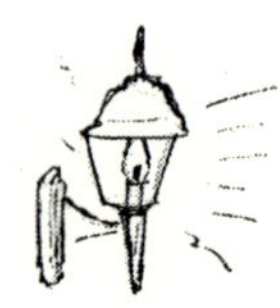

The Characteristics of a Vision

10

In the same way that you gave me a mission in the world,
I give them a mission in the world.

John 17:18 (MSG)

"What is a vision?"

My husband and I are different when it comes to money. He wanted to buy things I thought were outside our financial reach. I felt uncomfortable about getting deeper into debt. Our debts mounted and we had to spend more and more money just on interest payments and credit card bills. He was intuitive and big picture in his approach. I was more logical and detailed in my thinking.

I decided that I needed a different way of approaching this sensitive issue in our relationship. I sought to listen more and speak less. I sought to understand him before seeking to address the wisdom of a purchase decision. When he would say, "What if we had a new barbecue grill?" Instead of arguing with him I chose to listen and to understand him. I began to say, "Yeah, I think you're right, it would be nice to have a new grill. Let's see what would happen if we bought it. Let's look at all the pieces." Then I would bring out the budget and show the consequences of the purchase. He often came to the conclusion himself that we were better off not making the purchase.

We really began to come together in managing our finances when we began living out our family vision. Our vision keeps us both on track. Now we have a shared vision before us. We're now walking the same pathway, supporting each other, holding each other accountable as we make our financial decisions based on our vision. We consider whether or not potential purchases move us forward with our vision.

Your vision is the heartbeat of your family as it journeys with Jesus. Your vision distinguishes you from all other families in the world. If you don't know what makes your family unique then you will have no context or basis by which to make decisions, and you'll most likely make decisions based on how you feel or on what you are thinking in that moment.

In the Bible story of how God created Adam and Eve, God begins with the idea, saying, "*Let us make humankind in our image...,*" and so creating a spiritual reality.[67] Then God creates the physical reality of Adam and Eve. In the same way, we tune in our vision first as an idea and then as a reality that shows up in the physical world. Your vision begins as a spark, an image, an idea, a mental and spiritual reality. Then, as your family members commit to and live out your vision it becomes an emotional and physical reality. The spark for your vision usually begins within an individual as a personal idea or vision and then moves to the group as a whole, where it becomes shared with, affirmed, and shaped by, your whole family.

Some families, though not many, tune in their vision as a result of direct and specific revelation from God. Whether by special revelation or not, God provides the guidance you need to tune in your vision. Your vision will draw you closer to God, all creation, and to accomplishing what you were put on Earth as a family to do.

Every family's vision will look different. Your vision includes a **mission message** that quickly conveys the family's mission and a set of **core values and beliefs.** Keep in mind, how your family expresses these vision elements will look different, depending on the characteristics of your family, including its size, age-range, and structure.

Your vision will have the following characteristics:

A God-Focus

When your vision encourages your relationship with, and reliance on, God it aligns with what the Bible says and with Jesus' character, ministry, behavior, and words. Like a parent with a young adult child, God says, "*I have provided you with my guidance. You were born for such a time as this. Go and make wise decisions, knowing I am your resource—my presence is within you.*"

When your vision has a God focus, it aligns with the fact that the Bible invites us to know Jesus, hang out with him, become like him, and invite others to commit to Jesus as the leader of their lives and the forgiver of their souls.[68] The Bible says we are to be holy as God is holy, to love God with all our heart, soul, mind, and strength.[69] Growing into the character of Jesus, we will create and donate love and express joy, peace, patience, kindness, goodness, faithfulness, gentleness, and self-control.[70]

You receive guidance from God for wise decision-making through:

a) Meditating on what God says through the Bible;
b) Prayer—time hanging out with your leader;
c) God's presence and wisdom;
d) Research;
e) Seeking the suggestions of trusted others; and
f) Personal reflection.

Occasionally God provides special guidance. Receiving this special guidance is a gift and so I suggest that you not wait for it to be given you before you go forward with tuning in your vision. If it comes, celebrate and be grateful. If it does not come, celebrate and be grateful still!

You are not looking for the one vision which, if you do not discover and choose it, you will have missed what God wants for your family. You have freedom and choices from which to make wise decisions about the best vision for your journey now.

You have the guidance from God you need to make wise decisions in tuning in your vision. Whether you act on special or on general revelation, God fuels the vision you tune in as a family. Your vision shows up in your lives as an exclamation, "*Yeah God!*"

Balance

Your vision is balanced when it develops each of the aspects of faith, growth, mission, and nurture in your journey together as a thriving family (see chapter 6).

Phenomenal

Your vision is phenomenal when, while you can write and speak words to describe your vision, it cannot wholly capture the essence of this vision at work in your family. While your vision concerns you on a practical level it also has a magical, intangible quality hard to capture. The vision seems to capture you more than you the vision! Your vision is most fully expressed without words. Your vision is more a heartbeat than a document, more of a passion than a slogan, more a mindset than a series of tasks. Your vision inspires your relationship with Jesus and cultivates within you the same attitude that he has.

Energizing

Pondering your vision gives you goose bumps. Living it out with your leader energizes you. You enjoy knowing that you are aligned with something greater than yourself and in partnership with God in God's unfolding story for the world. What more magnificent a cause could be created for you than to partner with your creator for the world?

While your vision is big and you may grow weary, you rarely tire of the journey itself. Your vision challenges you to create and donate love between you as family members and for the world. Your vision energizes you to be a witness to others and lay the groundwork for God's unfolding story for the world. Your vision energizes you because it aligns you with your leader.

Fruitful

Living out your vision is not only exciting and meaningful for you but it also generates results in the unfolding story of God. The first ongoing result is that you become more like Jesus. The second ongoing result is that you contribute toward others becoming more like Jesus. The third ongoing result is that you donate love to a world hungry and thirsty for unconditional love.

If you were a fruit tree, living out your vision would be like growing deep and wide roots that drink life-giving water and then bear lots of fruit that animals and people eat. Seedlings from your tree spread in the wind and by animals eating your fruit. Other fruitful trees are born around you and where the animals hang out. These other fruitful trees themselves bear fruit and donate seeds for the wind and animals to spread throughout the land.

Your vision balances within you a rich inner life and an effective outer focus that impacts the lives of others. Your vision inspires and guides your family in becoming more like your leader. Your vision provides a basis from which you develop your own and others' leadership skills. As you spend more time hanging out with God, you become shaped by God more into the image of God and character of Jesus. As a result, you serve others. As a result of serving others, you develop a greater appreciation for the compassion, power, and movement of God. God shapes you through others, perhaps especially those you serve. As you engage God, God engages you for the world!

You take risks in living out your vision. Your vision becomes real only when you embody and express your vision with strangers. You have an inner urgency for your purpose on Earth and for the needs and lives of others. As a result of the risks you take—whether starting up a conversation in a coffee shop, at a soccer game, going on a mission to Haiti, Kenya, or Idaho, or offering an empathic ear to a friend who has lost her spouse or a child—you forever and practically impact the lives of others.

You provide water, food, shelter, and clothing. You donate love in ways that defy the win-lose nature of the world. You cause people to become curious because of your behavior and approach. You share with friends God's desire for relationship and how God makes that possible. Your vision inspires and guides your family on its journey to live with the same mind and heart that Jesus has for the world.

The vision you tune in as a family gives the most expressive "*yeah God!*" possible. The Bible says that this happens when you bear much fruit.[71] Bearing fruit means you grow in maturity as you spend time hanging out with God and you develop others who, like you, are growing in partnership with God in what God is doing for the world.

Measurable

While your vision and journey have great intangible qualities, you can also quantify your progress. Your family vision provides a means and basis for being accountable together on your journey. You move in unity with a common vision, so you know when you're out of sync, and when you've partnered with God in transforming people's lives.

By measurable, I don't mean the vision must have numerical components, though it can. For many, having a vision that includes, for example, "introducing nine families to Jesus in 2009" could tempt you to focus on numbers and not on relationships, including relationships with your leader. For some, such a numeric vision creates urgency, excitement, and focus.

You can easily determine your progress concerning your vision. The vision map described in chapter fifteen is an excellent tool for charting your progress. Your vision can be embodied in a tangible and measurable way. When you review your vision, and the milepost markers by which you will measure your movement with God, you will know whether you need more time hanging out with your leader, being active in your church, building relationships in the community, or nurturing your family's own relationships and bond together.

You can ask, "*How are we doing?*" and objectively get an answer. You can each look at a scoreboard, if you will, measuring your journey's results. In addition to measuring your progress in partnering with God, you can measure your progress in being a family that builds trust, masters conflict, achieves unity, embraces mutuality, and focuses on principles (see chapter 6). You can measure your progress in each of the faith, growth, mission, and nurture aspects. You can together see and measure your progress as you live out your vision. What a journey you are making!

Your vision is impossible—except with Jesus as your leader

Your vision is big—*bigger than you*. It's bigger than you can handle, except with Jesus as your leader.[72] Your vision inspires you to rely upon God who provides for your needs. God provides you the power, presence, and resources by which your vision supernaturally becomes possible. Were your vision left to you it would wither and die. It would not be a vision but an impractical idea that fails. While failure is an opportunity to learn and grow, why settle for failure when instead you can partner with God in God's unfolding story for the world?

Family Journey Point: Chapter Ten

To Ponder: When someone says to you, "Your family will have a dynamic vision powerfully shaping who you are," the reaction you have is...

To Consider: What if you were to weave your family's messy story into the unfolding story of God for the world? What would that look like?

To Remember: *"In the same way that you gave me a mission in the world, I give them a mission in the world."*

John 17:18 (MSG)

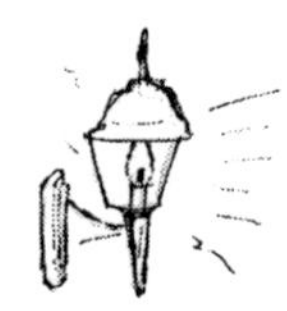

The Visioning Process

11

If people can't see what God is doing, they stumble all over themselves; but when they attend to what he reveals, they are most blessed.

Proverbs 29:18 (MSG)

"How do we tune in our vision?"

I was eight years old. Our phone rang. My mother answered.

She gave me the phone, saying, "It's for you."

"Hello?" I said as I took the phone.

"Can you come over and play today?" a familiar voice on the other end asked.

Always ready for fun playing with my friends, I replied, "Okay! I'll be over in a little while. Bye." I handed the phone back to my mother.

She asked, "Who was that?"

I thought for a moment, the realization sinking in for me, "I don't know." I didn't know whether that was my friend Bobby or George or another. I didn't know where I was going or which way to go! The questions you ask—and wrestle with—directly shape the direction and focus of your journey.

God is a high definition leader. God consistently and repeatedly sets out a clear, vivid and big vision (the biggest in existence) for God's followers and then gives lots of freedom and room—not to mention God's own power—for the followers in living out the vision.[73] In the same way, God gives lots of freedom and room for tuning in your own family vision.

The process for tuning in your vision is most exciting because, beyond nurturing your family's health and vibrancy, you are committing to making a difference in other people's lives. You are moving intentionally and actively with God weaving into the unfolding story of God for the world.

Your family's own process will vary depending on its size, age-range, and structure. While your vision will come from individuals, the visioning process is done as a group, as much as possible, in partnership and cooperation with God as your leader. The results of your visioning process will be in alignment with what God reveals to you through the Bible. The components of your vision may include the following:

- **Mission Message**
- **Core Values**
- **Core Beliefs**

Use these components to encourage your relationship with Jesus as leader of your family and to grow in your effectiveness in moving with him for the benefit of the world. For families with younger children, I suggest you tune in a vision even your younger children can understand and remember. As your children grow, you can adapt and tune in a new vision that fits their maturity. Involve your children as much as possible in tuning in your vision, even if at times by setting out paper and crayons so they can color while the older members tune in the vision.

Let's review in detail the characteristics of each vision component and how to tune them in.

Mission Message

"*So, tell me about your family?*" If you can't answer that question easily and naturally within a few seconds your family's mission message is not clear enough. And, you may have missed an opportunity to be a witness to an amazing love. Your mission message describes your universal purpose in common with every other family that follows Jesus.

What would it be like if what you say intrigues everyone within earshot and leads to deeper conversation and relationships? Your mission message is one among many ways of building relationships with others and being clear within your family about why you exist.[79] What you say is highly defined, concise, clear, unambiguous, warm, and bold. What you say expresses the essence of what energizes and excites you.

Your mission message should be based in reality and upon the shape of your family, its skills, background, interests, knowledge, experiences, and relationship with its leader. Your mission message is a sentence or phrase. The time-frame for this message can be anywhere between one and five years or longer. **The key question is, "*For what purpose (in three seconds or less) did God create your family?*"**

In general, the Biblical mission of families is to be an apprentice with Jesus, inviting and teaching as many people as possible in your circles of influence to follow him.

Example 1a: We follow Jesus for the world.

Example 1b: The Smith team follows Jesus for the world.

Example 1c: Following Jesus for the world.

Above are three ways of expressing essentially the same mission message for different needs or circumstances.

Creating your Mission Message
Ask yourselves, "For what purpose did God create our family?" There are potentially five pieces to the mission message: 1) Your family, 2) Jesus, 3) What you do, 4) Whom you seek to benefit, and 5) What the core benefit you provide is.

Below is the structure. The order of the four pieces is not set in stone, so feel free to adapt and move them around in creating your mission message.

________	________	________	________	________
Your family	Jesus	What you do	For whom	Core benefit

Fig. 3

Example 2:
With Jesus, we invite other young families in Little Rock to enjoy the good news

With Jesus, we invite friends in Little Rock to enjoy the good news

In this example, "With Jesus" is the family's connection with Jesus, "invite" is what the family does, "friends in Little Rock" or "other young families" is who they invite, and "enjoy the good news" is the core benefit (see Figure 3).

Example 3:
The Johnson family receives Jesus and gives back to the Ridgefield community

In this example, "receives Jesus" is the family's connection with Jesus; "gives back" is what it does; "the Ridgefield community" is for whom. This example does not explicitly state a core benefit.

Example 4:
The Jones family donates love and offers hope to the homeless.

In this example, Jesus is not explicitly named; "donates love" is what the family does, "the homeless" is for whom, "offers hope" is the core benefit.

Example 5:
We help our neighbors experience Jesus' love.

Helping our neighbors experience Jesus' love.

In this example, the family's connection with Jesus is referenced in the mention of "Jesus' love," "helping" is what the family does; "neighbors" is who they help, "experiencing Jesus' love" is the core benefit.

Example 6:
We follow Jesus by loving and learning from him and loving and leading like him

In this example, the family's main connection to Jesus is following him; loving, learning, and leading are what the family does; for whom isn't explicitly stated; and, "loving and leading like him" are the core benefits. See other examples in Appendix B.

You want your mission message to be:

- Clear
- Specific
- Concise
- Direct
- Transparent or open
- Memorable

Clarity defines. A clear message attracts results because it quickly and easily forms as a defined idea in the mind of its hearers and ideas are attractive. If your message is not clear then it loses its potential luster and ability to impact others. What is an unclear message? A message that has grammatical errors, is wordy, vague, uses past tense, and is loaded with the passive verb "to be" (such as "The Smiths are giving...." Instead, use "The Smiths give..." or "Giving...").

Being specific defines. Use messages that express a dimensional quality like "younger families" instead of "families" or "people." Shy away from using the word "people" in your message because it lacks specificity and dilutes your message. Instead, ask yourself "what sort of people am I talking about?"

Being concise defines. Such a message provides you the best opportunity to express and bring to mind an image of what you are saying. If you can use fewer words to convey the same message then the hearer has more time to establish an image in their own mind's eye. Winston Churchill got up to deliver his speech to graduating university students. He got up to the dais, settled in and said, "*Never give up! Never give up! Never give up!*" and sat down. His point was made. His hearers understood his message loud and clear.

Being direct defines. When tuning in their mission message, many struggle with being direct. We like to think that being indirect is polite, nice, inoffensive, and unassuming. Being "nice," however, is not the same as behaving well. In fact, being nice often is a way of hiding behind what's really going on inside us or in our relationships. Being nice is often what we do instead of being open and direct about our needs, motives, thoughts, feelings, and desires. Though perhaps you may go through a period of discomfort for putting yourself "out there," I think you'll become excited and empowered in defining your allegiance with Jesus and why you exist as a family for the world.

Here's an example—a family starts out saying, "We love people as best as we possibly can." This is too general a statement. People? What kind of people? Love? What's the source of, and motivation for, your love? As best you can? Sounds ambiguous and empty. The family eventually gets the idea and tunes in, "We help our neighbors experience Jesus' love."

You want to use simple active verbs (the simpler the better). Below are some examples:

- Give
- Create
- Develop
- Get
- Find
- Perform
- Manifest
- Train
- Teach
- Transform
- Change
- Heal

Help is often not an ideal word as it can convey an enabling relationship and can imply desperation on the part of those for whom you do what you do. If you use it, use it in a context where you engage with others who are usually strong, able, independent, and not needy. See Appendix C for more on brainstorming your message.

Three-Step Process

Let me suggest a three-step process for tuning in your mission message.[74] Using this process will generate ideas, promote family unity, and help you tune in the wisest option in alignment with God's guidance.

1. Preparing

In tuning in your family vision, what if each member personally made the following four commitments?:

1) Agree to allow God to be your leader. You may feel inadequate to the task of tuning in what God wants. That's okay. In fact, that's good. God works best when we make room for God within us. Pray something like this: "God, I'd like to know you better than I do. I want you to take over the leadership of my life. I'll follow and you lead. I want what you want for my life, even when I'm not clear about what that is. Guide me in going with the way of Jesus. I'm looking forward to the adventure! In Jesus' name, amen."

2) Seek to trust God's guidance. God loves us perfectly and perfectly desires what is good for us.[75] God is powerful beyond measure and yet also loving. God provides everything necessary to guide us. We reasonably can trust God's willingness and ability to guide. God wants us to know what God wants so we can obey and grow more like God in our behavior and character.

3) Seek to let go. Each person must become indifferent to all but what God wants. Being indifferent does not mean that you do not care. Rather being indifferent means you are open and focused above all on what God wants in such a time and situation as this. You do not abandon your own values and convictions but let go of them for the purpose of making room for God's guidance. Be convinced that what God wants is best. I find that hanging out with God best prepares me to let go and to tune in our vision. Quiet time fuels action time—the process of tuning in your vision. An excellent way to go about letting go is to practice centering prayer (see pages 54-55).

Acknowledge and intentionally set aside prejudgments about the vision. You want to have an open mind so as to be moved and shaped by the movement of God among you. Set aside even those prejudgments you believe are right. You cannot tune in your vision if you have your mind already made up before you begin.

4) As a family, agree to tune in your vision and live it out. Commit to God as the leader of your family and to tune in your vision and live it out. Each member of the family is equally important and valued. Each is uniquely shaped for serving others and creating love. When you are in agreement to be about tuning in your vision, God empowers your agreement and the journey you make in tuning in your vision.

When you commit together to the journey, the learning will be deeper, your sense of community more profound, your bonding will be strong and exciting and your family potential will be greater. When you commit together you will experience the power of united prayer as you tune in your vision and live it out. Disagreement or disharmony between you will disrupt your ability to hang out with God in prayer. When you can set aside your different concerns and your hearts beat as one then the presence of God is evident and people know that God is moving within and among you.

The commitment of children, especially those younger than three or four, will take a different form than that of teens and adults. Involve everyone as much as possible on the journey and in ways meaning for all.

The journey is not about uniformity but unity. Some may feel committing to the journey will confine them. Yet, the journey actually creates greater freedom, purpose, a liberating way of being family, and an environment that encourages creativity, ingenuity, and all you can bring to bear in living out your lives together.

2. Brainstorming Options

Let me suggest these steps for generating ideas for your mission message.

1) Check-in with each other. During this check-in process, listen for how God may be speaking through each person. This check-in time encourages everyone to feel connected as you get started. The key question is: How are each of you feeling as you prepare to tune in your vision and sharing any thoughts about the journey ahead. If you'd rather, ask: 1) What I am feeling most concerned about is ... 2) What I am most excited about is ....

2) Spend time hanging out with God together. Your prayer time could include using familiar songs or hymns, celebrative songs that laud God, songs of personal confession, and reading Bible passages. Ask God for the wisdom to make wise decisions together that honor God as you tune in your mission message.

With our toddlers and kindergartner, prayer often includes clapping for God, cheering out, "*Yeah God!*," being silent, dancing for God, playing an instrument for God—morracas, drums, tambourine, recorder—or high-fiving for God. Be creative and use your imagination.

As you hang out with God together you come clean before God. You experience and celebrate God together. You bathe yourselves in the presence and power of God as you express acclaim for God. Your desire to align with God increases. As your desire to align with God increases, you draw closer together as a family. This transformation happens not as you study, research, or talk about hanging out with God but as you actually hang out with God. Spending between five and thirty minutes or so in prayer at the beginning of family time together can bring your family into significantly greater alignment with your leader as you gather.

3) Dream. Re-imagine your family story in light of Jesus' leadership and begin to claim new hopes and dreams for your family. These dreams are your answers to these questions, "*During the next three years of following Jesus, what do we want to have accomplished? For what do we want to be known?*" You can also explore this question using the phrase, "A*t the end of our lives,*" or "*During the next five years...*". Write down and share your dreams with the others. Listen to each other's dreams without criticism or negative comment. If it helps, have each person go through the visioning exercise described in Figure 1 on page 53.

4) Reflect on Bible passages. Pray that God's presence guide your time together. Read Matthew 16:13-25. Have one or two people share responses to the question, "What phrases and ideas jumped out at you in this passage?" Have each person respond to the question, "Who is Jesus to you?"

Read from and reflect on Bible passages so you can cultivate alignment with what God reveals and wants for you. The passages may instruct, inspire, and shape you. See Appendix A for other suggested Bible passages.

5) Brainstorm Options. Become familiar with Figure 3 on page 130, "*Creating Your Mission Message,*" and with the mission message examples provided. Brainstorm options in alignment with what God reveals from the Bible. Use Appendix C as a worksheet to generate ideas, either before or during your family brainstorming session.

Hear this word of caution: Because words are powerful, take care in the words you choose, say, and use. This is a big responsibility, bringing into reality a focus to the point of seeking to have the reality show up in your life. Be sure your message aligns with what the Bible says. Be sure your message is positive and creates a positive result for everyone. Remember, you are seeking wise decisions for honoring God and that you are passionate about.

The brainstorming process is an intense idea-generating session holding in tension your family self-awareness and your awareness of God.[77] I suggest that each last no more than an hour. Appoint a facilitator and a note-taker for the brainstorming process. These brainstorming guidelines will guide you toward the best possible results (you may want to write them on poster board and hang them on a wall):

- **Defer judgment:** Don't dismiss any ideas;
- **Build on the ideas of others:** No "buts", only "ands";
- **Encourage wild ideas:** Embrace the most out-of-the-box notions because they may represent a key wisdom, insight, or revelation;
- **Go for quantity:** Aim for as many new ideas as possible. In a good session, up to 100 ideas are generated in sixty minutes;
- **Be visual:** For example, use different colored markers to write on big poster board taped to the wall;
- **Stay focused on the topic:** Always keep the discussion on target (acknowledge off-topic comments and defer them for later);
- **One conversation at a time:** No interrupting, dismissing, disrespect, or rudeness.

The note-taker writes down on a big paper on the wall all the ideas that are offered, so all can see them. The note-taker will later transfer them to a smaller size to keep long-term. The facilitator encourages the formation of ideas, the participation of all, and reminds others of the rules of brainstorming, when necessary.

6) Weigh the options brainstormed. Whittle down the list together to two to five of the options you most want to explore further. Wise decisions are not based on ignorance or apathy. Each person becomes informed about each option, examines the wisdom of each, weighing the pros and cons in living the option out. The more informed you are, the easier your decision-making becomes.

If you need help narrowing down the options, I suggest that you do the following:

- Together pray for wisdom for making wise decisions that honor God;
- Each person separately lists and prioritizes their top seven options;
- Identify which options were selected most, and of those, add together the scores for each (tally one point for each top priority choice, two for each second choice, and so on). The lower the score, the higher-rated the option;
- If you do not yield as many as five options then identify which options were selected second most between you all;
- Go through the same process with those until you have up to five options to explore further.

For example, let's say you have three family members. Let's also say that you each have two options in common on each of your top-seven lists. You would then tally up the points for each of those two options to determine which was your top option and which was your second option. Let's say that two of you have three options in common among your top seven. You would then tally up the points for each of those three options to determine which was your third, fourth, and fifth options.

3. Tuning in Your Mission Message

1) Each person reflects on the narrowed list of options and prepares reasons for supporting each option. In this good-upon-good approach, no weaknesses are pointed out. Each person prays silently about the options, looking only for the good in each. She writes down reasons for supporting each option.

2) The family gathers again and each person presents their reasons for supporting each option. Each names the good they see in each option. Good is added to good. One of you serves as a facilitator and asks each person to name the good they see in each option, their reasons for supporting each option (it's a good idea to have a rule against rebuttal and debate at this point, to ensure that all feel free to express themselves). Questions are allowed only for clarification. When you eliminate debate, this process of listening to, receiving, and understanding each other's reasons will open the way for new light to shine, without pitting one person's ego or will against another's.

If one family member says, "*God revealed this to me,*" then be sure to ask them to define and explain their revelation. Then ask the family if they are comfortable with receiving what the member says as a revelation. If the revelation is not from God, then you will find the member is hiding behind what they say by cloaking their statement with a false authority. If the revelation is from God, the tuning in process will prove it true.

3) Each person reflects alone on the reasons presented and prepares her conclusion. Each person weighs the reasons for each option against the others and assesses which is weightier. Each may ask in their time alone, "*Which reason expresses the greatest wisdom for our situation? Which option draws us closer to God and leads to our fullest participation with God?*" Then each person prepares their conclusions.

4) The family gathers again and each person presents his or her prayerful conclusion. Once again, there is to be no debate. You do not want to pit one person's will, ego, debating ability against another's. Discussion and questions are allowed for clarification only.

5) Choosing your mission message. The family votes, seeking the wisest decision that most draws it close to God and most effectively guides it in living and sharing God's story for the world. The facilitator's role is to mirror to the group what may be emerging as a consensus for direction. By consensus, I do not mean that all members vote for the same option. I mean those who did not vote with the majority consent to going along with the majority. They agree to make it a unanimous vote.

If a vote is almost evenly divided, I do not press for consensus. Instead, go back in the process of tuning in your vision.

Take your time through this step of choosing your vision. Disagreement in this process may be the presence and wisdom of God speaking to your family through these individuals. If one person or a few people refuse to change their vote, then go back and continue in the process of tuning in your vision. Ask your family to prayerfully reflect on the statements and conclusions of others and prepare another assessment. Continue the process until consensus emerges or your family feels it has gone as far as it can or runs out of time.

If you disregard viewpoints on the minority side of a vote you risk inflicting great injury in your family and sowing seeds of division.

The facilitator often expresses a "trial balloon," a summary statement based on family input that expresses where the family seems prayerfully to be led. However, someone else may be the one to advance this trial balloon to the family. Family members may then be asked to show their level of support for the trial balloon. This can be gauged through conversation or a show of hands of how many are supportive.

Once you have tuned in your mission message, high five, cheer, pray with thanks and gratitude for your leader's guidance!

Core Values

These express what your family sees as important under Jesus' leadership and guidance. Your core values statement may be one sentence or a sentence plus a list of three to five bulleted phrases. The time frame may be anywhere between one to five years or longer. **The key question is, "*What are our priorities as Jesus leads and guides our family?*"**

Example 1:
The Smith team values donating love *(1 John 4:15-17)*, seeking truth *(John 14:6)*, and growing more like Jesus *(Ephesians 4:13)*.

Example 2:
The Jones team rules are be kind, be safe, and be respectful.

Example 3:
The Johnson team values being wise managers of resources *(Psalm 24:1)*, learning more about the Bible *(2 Timothy 3:15-17)* , serving others *(Mark 10:45)*, and making followers of Jesus *(Matthew 28:18-20)*.

Two-Step Process

Now you are ready to tune in your core values in light of this newly tuned in mission message. Once again, you are seeking to tune in the wisest option in alignment with God's guidance.

Brainstorming Options

1) Pray. Pray something like, "Dear God, you are great, loving, compassionate, and awesome. We're grateful that you are our leader. Give us your wisdom so that we can make wise decisions about our core values that are in alignment with you. In Jesus' name, amen."

2) Brainstorm Options. Become familiar with the basic structure of the three examples of core values above. Brainstorm options in alignment with what God reveals from the Bible. Use the brainstorming guidelines outlined in the mission message section above. At this point, do not concern yourself with creating your whole core values sentence. Focus instead only on brainstorming your core values themselves.

Remember to have a note-taker write down all the ideas that are offered, so all can see them. Remember also to have one of you serve as a facilitator to encourage the formation of ideas, the participation of all, and to remind others of the rules of brainstorming, when necessary.

3) Weigh the options brainstormed. Whittle down the list together to five options you most want to explore further. I suggest that you do the following:

- Each person separately lists and prioritizes their top five options;
- Identify which options were selected most, and of those, add together the scores for each (tally one point for each top priority choice, two for each second choice, and so on). The lower the score, the higher-rated the option;
- If you do not yield as many as five options then identify which options were selected second most between you all;
- Go through the same process with those until you have five options to explore further.

For example, let's say you have four family members. Let's also say that you each have three options in common on each of your lists. You would then tally up the points for each of those three options to determine which was your top option, and which was your second and third options. Let's say that two of you have two options in common among your separate lists. You would then tally up the points for each of those two options to determine which was your fourth and fifth options.

Tuning in Your Core Values

1) Each person reflects on the list of five options and prepares reasons for supporting each option. In this good-upon-good approach, no weaknesses are pointed out. Each person prays silently about the options, looking only for the good in each. She writes down reasons for supporting each option.

2) The family gathers again and each person presents their reasons for supporting each option. At this point, resist the urge to make comparisons between proposed core values.

3) Each person reflects alone on the reasons presented and prepares his conclusion. Each person now weighs the reasons for each option against the others and assesses which is weightier. Each may ask in their time alone, "*Which reason expresses the greatest wisdom for our situation? Which option draws us closer to God and leads to our fullest participation with God?*" Then each person prepares his own list, rating each option in order, from most preferred to least.

4) The family gathers again and each person presents his or her prayerful conclusion. Once again, there is to be no debate. You do not want to pit one person's will, ego, and debating ability against another's.

5) Choosing your core values. If you have three options in common between you then you have tuned in your core values and can create your core values sentence, "The Smith team values...." If you do not have three options in common, then see if you can reach agreement about which option to join with those you *do* have in common so as to tune in three core values. If you cannot reach agreement, then consider going back in the process until consensus emerges or your family feels it has gone as far as it can or runs out of time. Once you have tuned in your core values, high five, cheer, pray with thanks and gratitude for your leader's guidance!

Core Beliefs

These may be called core beliefs, beliefs, or core commitments. Core beliefs characterize how you uniquely live out your core values. The time frame may be anywhere between one to five years or longer. The key question is, "*How do we uniquely live out our core values?*"

Example 1: The Johnson family lives out our Core Values by living by these core beliefs: Jesus is the leader of our family; everything belongs to God; and, everyone belongs to God.

Example 2: The Randall family lives out our Core Values by living by these core beliefs: Around-the-clock worship of God; learning about God from the Bible; intentionally inviting friends into relationship with Jesus; and, using our talents.

Example 3: The Trundell family lives out our Core Values by living by these core beliefs: Jesus is our savior and leader; intentional apprentice-making, we each are gifted for serving.

Tuning in Your Core Beliefs

Now you are ready to tune in your core beliefs in light of both your newly tuned in mission message and core values. Use the same process as for tuning in your core values, described above.

Once you have tuned in your vision, keep your vision ever before you. Post it on your refrigerator, place it in your daily planner, and begin living it out. You can use any combination of components in writing to remind you and direct you day-to-day. For example, you could post your mission message, values, and beliefs on one page on your refrigerator. You could recite your mission message, values, and beliefs at family gatherings. You could place your mission message on letterhead, email signatures, family newsletters, baseball caps, and tee shirts. Remember, however, your vision is not birthed until you share and embody it with strangers.

Family Journey Point: Chapter Eleven

To Ponder: How can we learn about what God wants for us? Share your ideas and thoughts with each other.

To Consider: Commit to preparing, both personally and as a family, to tuning in your vision.

To Remember: *"If people can't see what God is doing, they stumble all over themselves; but when they attend to what He reveals, they are most blessed."*

Proverbs 297:18 (MSG)

Principle #5: The High Definition Family

... Let us love ... with actions and in truth

— **1 John 3:18** (NIV)

12 Living out the Vision

But you will receive power when the Holy Spirit comes on you; and you will be my witnesses in Jerusalem, and in all Judea and Samaria, and to the ends of the earth.

Acts 1:8 (NIV)

"What does it look like for us on a daily basis?"

On Sunday, as we drove to church, there was a man standing on the street corner with a cardboard sign asking for prayer and money. We discussed with our twin toddler boys and our five-year-old daughter in the car about our basic belief that everyone belongs to God and explored what we might do for this man.

The man was at a busy intersection two blocks from our church. We parked at church and Sayer ran back to talk with him. Sayer stayed only briefly because he knows that standing around and talking for too long is "bad for business"—he wouldn't be given any money by anyone else while Sayer visited with him.

Sayer learned his name is Andrew and more about his story. Andrew recited Jeremiah 29:11 and said, "I am hopeful because God has plans for me."

Sayer spoke a few words of encouragement and asked, "What do you want us to pray about for you?" He prayed with Andrew, gave a small amount of money, and joined us at church. That night we prayed as a family for Andrew.

Several days later while tucking our children into bed, I asked our children, "Who needs our prayer?"

"An-doo," replied Nathan. None of us understood.

"Andoo," he said again. Still, we puzzled at what he was saying. "Andoo," he persisted. Then we got it: Andrew.

You are on your God-guided, God-sized mission! You are moving forward with a compelling vision. You are aligning with what you've been created to be and do on Earth. Your vision re-imagines your old story, breathing new life and meaning into the challenges you have faced. Every aspect of your life will be shaped and directed by your vision: the nurture of your own family, your faith, personal growth, and mission. Every decision you face will be shaped, directed, and inspired by your vision. Your vision itself points back to your relationship with your leader. Your leader is the source of your guidance, power, inspiration, understanding, wisdom, compassion, and love. God is why you can re-imagine your story and here a little, there a little, live it out in a new and powerful way.

Your family vision is the basis for what your top priorities will be in the next few months. The decisions you make are made so as to advance your family vision. You gather every three to six months to review your progress, and your focus for the days and weeks ahead. You know what your goals are and your progress in achieving them. You know where you are and where you are going and have the freedom to journey engaging your family, wisdom, abilities, shape, passion, and leader as you go.

Your vision invigorates you—you feel like nobility and yet serve humbly. You have a new basis, a new compass, by which you are directed and make decisions. When you are deciding where to take a vacation, you ask yourselves something like, "*What can we do during our vacation time that best aligns with and advances our vision?*" When you are deciding where to shop, you ask yourselves, "*Where and how can we shop that most wisely embodies our vision?*" Perhaps you think about saving money so as to have more for other purposes. Perhaps you think about using re-usable bags and finding the closest store so as to leave as small a carbon footprint as possible and to minimize plastic at waste landfills. Perhaps you look for organics, or a store at which you can do one-stop shopping instead of just groceries. Whatever the case, you will ask, "*In the task of shopping, how can we most wisely and powerfully advance our vision?*"

You mention and refer to your vision every day, perhaps dozens or more times. As you reflect on, think, and talk about your vision all sorts of perspectives and opportunities open to you which perhaps otherwise would not have manifested. As you own your vision you move more fully with hope than fear. Setbacks on your way become hurdles rather than dream-breakers. You approach every road-block with a question –"*how can I use this to further the vision*"–rather than a sigh of defeat. You have a perspective forever stretched by God, moving with confidence in the greater story and movement of God for the world.

Your conflicts with others, both within your family and in your other circles of influence, have a new context – your vision and relationship with Jesus as your leader. Conflict becomes an opportunity rather than a dreaded fight to avoid. You have new tools and a new context for more confidently, humbly, and openly engaging others with the anticipation of new understanding, an opportunity to gift others with your understanding of them and asserting your needs. In conflict, you see an opportunity to learn, grow, more deeply understand, nurture relationships, and honor yourself and others.

Who will make dinner tonight? Who will take the kids to the library? Who will meet the plumber at the house at 2 p.m.? How much should we withdraw from savings to cover the dental bill? The details of life have a new canvas upon which to be expressed and lived out. You no longer see the small stuff as small but as an opportunity to bring about your vision. In every moment, person, relationship, transaction, detail, and project you have eyes for living out your vision. In everything you live with a sense of meaning, urgency, and purpose.

Your relationships with others in your circles of influence –acquaintances, friends, and strangers–are oriented into the context of your relationship with God. All belong to God. You have at least an inkling of how passionate God is for you and so also for them.[78] You ask yourself, "*What can I do, how can I be with my friend so as to best embody our vision with him and contribute to his own story and journey on this planet?*"

Your vision provides the basis for how you budget your money. A friend or stranger can review your checkbook and see what is important to you. Your vision directs you in allocating your budget toward furthering your vision. You are more and more spending money in ways aligned with your vision.

Your vision nurtures your faith as you are accountable to your vision in how you spend time hanging out with Jesus and in reading, studying, or meditating on, the Bible. Your faith journey comes to life as it weaves into your vision.

Your vision reminds and directs you every day to nurture your own self-care and personal growth.

> *I had put our toddler boys down for a nap. Our daughter was away visiting grandparents for a few days. Heidi, my wife, was away at a client's office. I had a choice between eating lunch at the usual time or spending quiet time, about an hour, hanging out with Jesus. I knew that if I didn't choose to hang out with Jesus then I would not have an opportunity until after the kids were in bed and even then I'd be tired. As I wrestled with the decision, I reviewed our family vision: following Jesus. and knew I wanted time*

with him. After my quiet time, the boys woke up and I ate a late lunch.

Every day your vision propels your mission. Your mind actively searches for opportunity. You may find opportunity in a wheelchair-bound person needing a hand at the store, a neighbor stopping to say hi, a conversation with a parent at a youth basketball game, lunch with a colleague, a church mission trip, or in inviting neighbors to a fun church event. You also begin creating ideas: leaving flowers at a neighbor's front door as a surprise, having a block party to get acquainted with neighbors, buying a newspaper subscription from a news carrier and telling him to have the paper delivered to a neighbor or friend, planning a trip to another area to provide free labor to renew a house, a church, or community center.

Every day your vision encourages an environment of nurture within your family. Your vision reminds you to take time to put "*special*" back into your "special relationships." Your vision inspires you to be a family continually seeking to nurture each other, donate love, and to cause your family members to smile. You remind each other of your vision and regularly create ideas for embodying and expressing your vision. You share with each other the results of ways you've moved with, or have seen, God's movement for the world. You share stories about what has and has not worked.

You begin to weave the story of your journey and the stories of the Bible together as you live out your vision. You talk about the Bible in relation to your daily lives—a Bible conversation. You read from the Bible and talk about it, exploring how it is relevant to your lives. You see how your journey and God's are coming together. Everything you do you assess against your vision for alignment and more powerfully and joyfully moving forward with each other and with God for the world.

Family Journey Point: Chapter Twelve

To Ponder: Reflect on a time when you had an idea for a project and then did something about it, putting it into action. What did you do that helped bring about the good result?

To Consider: Commit to living out your family vision.

To Remember: *You will receive power when the Holy Spirit comes on you; and you will be my witnesses in Jerusalem, and in all Judea and Samaria, and to the ends of the earth.*

Acts 1:8 (NIV)

Family Gatherings

... In Christ we who are many form one body, and each member belongs to all the others.

Romans 12:5 (NIV)

13

"Why do we need family gatherings?"

We all sat down for dinner. It was early Sunday evening. "Who are we?," I asked.

"The Johnson team!," everyone yelled out, including our four-year-old boy and seven year-old daughter .

What's our vision?," Donna asked.

"To follow Jesus!" we all exclaimed.

"What do we believe?" I asked.

"Be safe. Be loving. Be 'spectful," replied our four-year-old.

"Okay. Good job – those are our rules (our values). How about our beliefs?" I replied.

"I know," piped up our seven-year old, "Jesus is our leader. Everybody and everything belongs to God!"

"Good job!" said Donna.

"You know, Jesus spent lots of time praying. Does anyone want to lead our prayer time tonight?"

"I do! I do!" yelled both of our kids.

The trouble with meetings is they tend to be boring and unproductive, take a long time, and sap our energy. In addition, meetings tend to attract a melting pot of different needs that easily overwhelm the expectations, structure, and time-frame of any meeting. Why have meetings and subject your family to the tedium, boredom, waste, energy-sapping ritual? Why do we need that? *You don't!* I suggest what we do need is life-giving drama and a focused gathering purpose. And family gatherings are where you can engage and celebrate in life-giving drama and gather with purpose.

Life-Giving Drama

Having tuned in your vision you have not only begun to intentionally re-imagine your future but have tuned in a life-giving tension—your old story begins to be re-told and re-imagined, woven into the fabric of your emerging new story. God accepts us just as we are, old story and all. Then God says, "*I am doing a new thing in you and am empowering you in re-imagining your lives and your story.*" This tension created by tuning in your vision sets the stage for life-giving drama in your family. Gradually, day by day, here a little, there a little, our old story is used and woven into a new story. Notice what happens with this family's story in the Bible.

> *Jacob settled with his family in his father's old stomping grounds of Canaan. Jacob, together with his wives Leah, Rachel, Leah's maid Zilpah, and Rachel's maid Bilhah, had twelve sons.*
>
> *Joseph, seventeen years old, a son by Rachel, helped out with his brothers herding their flocks. His brothers were his half-brothers, actually, the sons of Bilhah and Zilpah. Joseph brought his father bad reports on them. Jacob favored Joseph over his other sons because he was a child of his old age. Jacob had a fancy coat made for him. When Joseph's brothers saw younger Joseph parading around in this special coat, they became furious. They would not speak with him.*

Joseph had a dream. When he told it to his brothers, they hated him even more. He said of his dream, "Listen. We were all out in the field gathering bundles of wheat. All of a sudden my bundle stood straight up and yours circled around and bowed down to mine."

His brothers said, "So! You're going to rule us? You're going to boss us around?" And they hated him more than ever because of his dream and the way he talked. After sharing yet another dream, his brothers were stewing in jealousy and his father brooded in worry.

His brothers plotted to kill him. When they spotted him arriving in the field, they said, "Here comes that dreamer! Let's kill him and throw him into one of these old cisterns; we can say a vicious animal ate him up. We'll see what his dreams amount to."

When Joseph reached his brothers, they ripped off the fancy coat, grabbed him, and threw him into a dry cistern. They sat down to eat their supper. Looking up, they saw a caravan of Ishmaelites on their way from Gilead to sell their wares in Egypt. Judah said, "Brothers, what are we going to get out of killing our brother and concealing the evidence? Let's sell him to the Ishmaelites instead." His brothers agreed, selling Joseph to the Ishmaelites for twenty pieces of silver. The Ishmaelites took Joseph with them down to Egypt.

The brothers took Joseph's fancy coat, butchered a goat, and dipped the coat in the blood. They took the bloodied coat to their dad and said, "We found this. Look it over—do you think this is your son's coat?"

He recognized the coat at once. "My son's coat—a wild animal has eaten him. Joseph torn limb from limb!" Jacob tore his clothes in grief and distress.
In Egypt the Ishmaelites sold Joseph to Potiphar, one of

> *Pharoah's officials, manager of his household affairs. As it turned out, God was with Joseph and things went well with him. He ended up living in the home of his Egyptian master. His master saw that God was working for good in everything he did.*
>
> *Joseph had correctly interpreted Pharoah's dream of seven years of plenty and seven of famine. Joseph managed the years of plenty so as to see all of Egypt through the seven years of famine. Pharoah said, "Isn't this the man we need? Are we going to find anyone else who has God's spirit in him like this?" So Pharoah commissioned Joseph, saying, "I'm putting you in charge of the entire country of Egypt."*
>
> *Joseph's brothers, suffering through famine in Canaan, sought to buy supplies from Egypt. They came before Joseph, not recognizing him, he having matured into an adult in a foreign land, and asked to buy provisions. Joseph ordered their sacks be filled with grain, their money be put back in their sacks, and they be provided rations for the road.*
>
> *Joseph, re-imagining his family story, told them, "I am your brother whom you sold into slavery in Egypt. God sent me here ahead of you to save your lives. You planned evil against me but God used those same plans for good, as you see all around you right now—life for many people."*[79]

The old story of Jacob's family was woven into the fabric of a new story. "*You planned evil against me but God used those same plans for good,*" says Joseph. The story of a dysfunctionally-behaving family became re-imagined and shaped into a new story carrying out God's purposes for good. No matter how dysfunctional or broken your story, in tuning in your vision and living it out you begin a journey of re-imagining your story within the story of God's movement for the world.

Being comfortable with conflict in the process of debating ideas and making decisions is important to re-imagining your family story. What if you encourage this type of conflict? What if you affirm each other as you boldly engage each other about the best course of action to take? Life-giving drama often comes from out of a willingness to engage in conflict about ideas, options, and decisions you face.

Family gatherings are the glue that make your vision stick in your lives together. Gatherings tell and shape your story and re-tell and re-shape your story as you make your way along your journey. If you do not regularly gather together your lives remain stuck in the same story, prone to react to the stresses of life. As you gather you will experience transformation as you proactively engage each other, your leader, and your vision. Choosing to gather regularly, you re-imagine your God-guided future.

Gatherings Focused for Moving with God

Meetings can quickly become a mixed-soup of different and competing agendas. You don't reach for a Phillips screwdriver when you need a flathead. You don't ask for a hammer when you need a small clamp. Why ask gatherings to do every job and get unproductive tedium, or at best, unmanageable chaos instead? Why not have specific gathering tools and gatherings for specific purposes?

A gathering to talk about your plans for the day is different from one addressing what your family's strategic goals will be. Spending time in checking in with each other at a deep, spiritual, and emotional level is very different from spending time in resolving a practical problem.

When you can be aware of the different gathering tools you have at your disposal and the specific purposes they serve then you can make clear what your guidelines are for any gathering. When you are in agreement on your focus, you can better honor each other, your different needs, and more powerfully move with God for the world. Your family gatherings can be both exciting and focused, serving both the needs of your family and of the world.

Family Journey Point: Chapter Thirteen

To Ponder: When I think about our family having a gathering, I have this reaction... Share your feelings and thoughts.

To Consider: What if you intentionally and regularly gathered as a family?

To Remember: *"...In Christ we who are many form one body, and each member belongs to all the others."*
Romans 12:5 (NIV)

Six Modes of Family Gatherings

14

But you will receive power when the Holy Spirit comes on you; and you will be my witnesses in Jerusalem, and in all Judea and Samaria, and to the ends of the earth.

Acts 1:8 (NIV)

"What is an effective family gathering?"

It had been a rough day. Our kids had spent the day with a sitter. They wanted to be with their parents. Though that day we were working at home, we were hard at work with pressing deadlines and were not available to our kids until dinnertime. I finished my work for the day and made dinner. We sat down and ate together. Our kids took their baths.

Our daughter Emma especially was feeling upset at a lack of attention from us. Emma locked herself into the bathroom and was screaming with anger and frustration. Our kids wanted attention and time with us. Heidi asked our daughter, "Can we talk?"

Emma replied, "No talky, talky!!"

Heidi and I agreed we needed to be in nurturing mode with them, helping them process their feelings and needs. So we put off bedtime and set out crayons and paper and began some healing play. As they colored, Emma opened up—and her parents slowed down—and she and we were able to explore her feelings and her needs. We each drew pictures and gave one to each other. We could have gone to bed that evening on time, but with lingering division and hurt. Instead, we experienced profound healing and laughter.

Effective family gatherings have different purposes for different gatherings. The family in these gatherings will be functioning in one of six modes: **managing, leading, nurturing, learning, enjoying, or worshiping.** Let's take a look at each way of being family and the behaviors that cultivate them.

Managing

Being in managing mode means you are creating order out of chaos. You have the pieces to the puzzle and now are arranging them into order. You are determining how to carry out your vision, activity, idea, project, or trip. Then you do it. You are more in left-brain, or logical, reasoning, practical mode. You are looking for practical answers rather than powerful questions or ideas. You are thinking about how to accomplish a goal rather than creating one. Without the benefit of managing mode, your family life would be unmanageably chaotic.

Leading

Being in leading mode means you are dissatisfied with what is and see what could be. You see opportunity where others see trouble. You see direction where others see location. You see how your family could be oriented and structured so as to reach its potential. You seek out how God is leading and moving and long to be part of God's movement. You want your family to be on the front lines of what God is doing, even right in your own neighborhood. You can identify the problems in how you and your family think and behave that limit its ability to participate with God and reach its potential. You can see solutions for the problem. You can identify the needs in your circles of influence you can meet. You see, and want to bring about, the big picture in your lives. Without the benefit of leading mode, your family would crawl along reacting to life, making important whatever screams loudest in your circumstances.

Nurturing

Being in nurturing mode, you take a proactive stance in walking with others and encouraging their own growth and well-being. You are willing to experience pain to bring someone else out of theirs. You see souls where others see bodies. You are able to go deeper in conversation and presence with another so as to be present with them in a most profound and nurturing way.

You are sensitive to others' emotions and state-of-being. You can sense when another is suffering or in pain, even if a silent pain. You are willing to still yourself so as to understand and receive another. You listen to others in such a way that they sense that you hear and understand them. You paraphrase what others say to you so as to check for whether you've understood them. You continue to do so until they agree you understand them. You know that everyone has their own perspective, journey and experience of the world.

Learning

When in learning mode, you are curious, a sponge for better understanding and knowledge. Rather than feel threatened by someone asking questions, you are thrilled and tickled someone asks. You are able to apply what you learn in meaningful ways. What you learn shapes who you are. You celebrate learning and how it can shape your life and the lives of others. Being in learning mode, you ask questions and seek answers, options, theories, ideas, philosophies, and understandings. The best teachers are those who love being in learning mode.

Enjoying

Being in enjoying mode, you are playful, in the moment, open, free, and unworried about how others perceive you. You draw others out and include them in the fun. You induce laughter in others. You are light-hearted and do not take yourself or circumstances too seriously. You understand God is in control of the big picture and are tickled to be part of God's plan. You can laugh in dire situations, bringing a spark of light into darker moments and moving your family forward where once it was stuck.

Worshiping

You enjoy God all the time. You have been transformed by God and so are humbled by, and in awe of, God. You enjoy singing or thinking about your relationship with God whether you are making a hundred two-sided copies of a set of IRS instructions or sitting in the front pew of the Washington National Cathedral. You worship throughout the day, sometimes as a family at home. You worship God in how you approach your family gathering time. You often express gratitude and joy in every cell of your being. Worship for you doesn't start and end but joyously goes forever on. You can be in worship mode while washing the dishes as easily as praying together as a family or in devoting time as a family to worship.

Different Modes for Different Tasks

Although these modes of being constantly compete with each other for your time, it can be helpful to look at how they pair with each other. Many families fall into managing mode at the expense of leading mode. Enjoying mode often overshadows nurturing mode. Most families are challenged by their busy schedule choices and competing interests and don't receive as much of the benefit of learning mode and worshiping mode. Look at the illustration below and notice the tension between the different modes of being as a family.

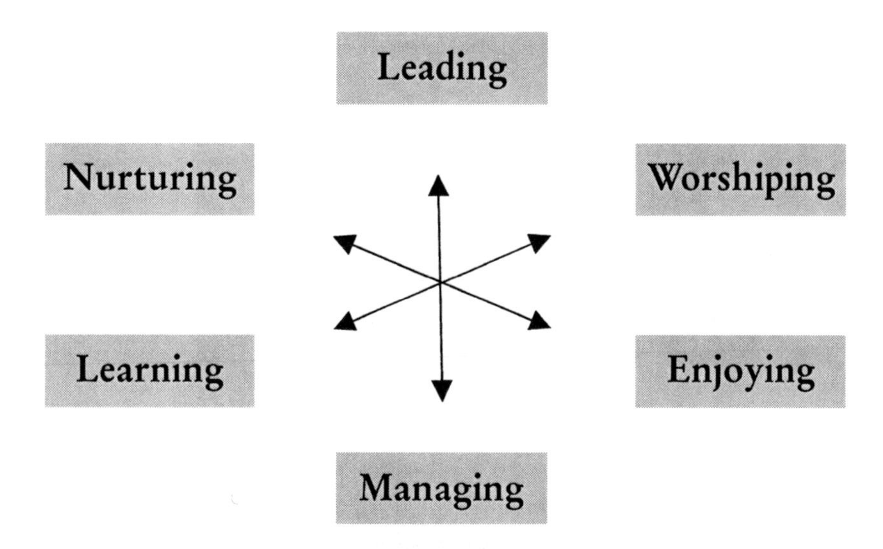

The tension between managing and leading modes: In managing mode you sense danger while in leading mode you see opportunity. In managing mode you follow procedures, while in leading mode you pursue visions. In managing mode you search for solutions while in leading mode you identify problems. In managing mode you serve your family while in leading mode you serve others. In managing mode you maximize what you have while in leading mode you cooperate with God in bringing about what you don't tangibly have. In managing mode you design incremental strategies while in leading mode you lay out sweeping strategies.[80]

The tension between enjoying and nurturing modes: In enjoying mode you see beauty outside of yourselves while in nurturing mode you see beauty inside of yourselves. In enjoying mode you seek pleasure while in nurturing mode you give pleasure. In enjoying mode you laugh; in nurturing mode you embrace. In enjoying mode you play with each other; in nurturing mode you listen to each other. In enjoying mode you share with each other while in nurturing mode you empathize with one another. In enjoying mode you make friends with joy, laughter, and giggles while in nurturing mode you make friends with pain, struggle, growth, and discovery.

The tension between learning and worshiping modes: When in learning mode we seek facts, figures, knowledge, and understanding; in worshiping mode we seek God. In learning mode we think, absorb, reflect, assess, and compare. When in worshiping mode, while we can think, reason, and reflect as we worship, we more often at core will praise, adore, enjoy, clap, sing, and receive. In learning mode we are moved in our mind. In worshiping mode we are moved in every way, including heart, soul, and being.

Choosing Your Mode for Your Purpose

Recognizing which mode is best for which purpose is important to being effective. If you are planning the details of a vacation trip to Disneyland then you want to be primarily in managing mode and secondarily, in enjoying mode. If you are assessing your vision together then you want to be primarily in leading mode and perhaps secondarily in managing mode. I suggest for every gathering, either before or during, you decide what the purpose of the gathering is and then which mode you want to be in. By acknowledging the mode that best suits your gathering needs you can facilitate your gathering more clearly and achieve a more powerful result. You can put on the hat or mode that best facilitates your purpose.

When you match a mode and your behavior with your gathering purpose you will experience more productive, dynamic family gatherings in line with your vision.

Family Journey Point: Chapter Fourteen

To Ponder: Which mode does my family express most often? Which does it express least? Share your thoughts.

To Consider: What if you were to intentionally use and grow in each of the six modes for family gatherings?

To Remember: *"While they were praying, the place where they were meeting trembled and shook. They were all filled with the Holy Spirit..."*

Acts 4:31 (MSG)

Twelve Tools for Family Gatherings

15

I want us to help each other with the faith we have.
Your faith will help me, and my faith will help you.

Romans 1:12 (NCV)

"Will this work for us?"

We (Joe and Kristin) were thrilled to be able to spend time with their nephew Caleb, 8, and niece Briana, 11. Their parents dropped them off. We had a day and a half to hang out together. Like most siblings close in age, they had lots of fun together but could also fight and be difficult with each other. Kristin and I (Joe) had been married almost two years, didn't have any children of our own, and were looking forward to being with them. We were excited at the opportunity to learn from them, be challenged by them, and to nurture our relationship with them. We started out playing competitive games, but this seemed to exacerbate conflict between Caleb and Briana.

So we changed our approach: creating a space for cultivating cooperative teamwork, trust-building, self-esteem, camaraderie, and a new harmony in our relationships together.

We decided to walk down to the neighborhood park. We spotted a play structure with bars, wood platforms, and hanging chain-links in a sand pit. We created a new game and set out the rules: you must follow the leader and you must not touch the sand. We readied ourselves to get started. "Oh, and, this is a team event," I said. "You must be in continual contact with the person in front of you." Briana and Caleb were very active in their schools and community academically and athletically. Both were top students and competitive. Yet this was unlike any game they had ever played.

I led our group, hopping up onto the play structure, weaving through the bars, walking along the swaying chain-links, along a balance beam, and all over the apparatus. The task was made difficult by the requirement we stay in physical contact with each other and not touch the sand. Briana was in contact with me, Caleb with Briana, and Kristin with Caleb. The whole exercise was difficult. Very difficult; it required communication and strong teamwork. We were exhilarated with the game and the bonding between us as we had fun with it.

We ended up doing many activities that weekend. But when Briana and Caleb's father came to pick them up the next day and Briana first saw her dad she excitedly exclaimed, "Dad! Guess what we got to do! We played this team game at the park!" and told him all about it.[81]

You use a hammer to pound a nail into wood, a measuring tape to measure with, a clamp to clamp two items together tightly. Why not use the tool you need for accomplishing specific tasks in your family gatherings? By mastering and having at your disposal a dozen different tools in your family gathering tool belt, you can ensure being effective, focused, and dynamic in meeting the family's needs and living out your vision. Here are twelve tools for family gatherings.

1. Hot Potato Huddle

This is a quick go-around where each member reports in one minute or less their plans for the day or the week, what excited them most about the day (especially useful if you have younger children), or what they like best about a given option in a decision the family faces.[82] This is a quick move-around-the-table survey to get a sense for what is going on for your family. If used separately without other tools, you may even want to have everyone stand as though in a huddle so as to reinforce the intention to keep it brief. It's a way of checking-in together quickly and getting a read on where everyone is. Use your imagination in applying this tool. You can use it to get a read on what's developing in the week ahead, to emotionally check-in quickly and simply, to validate everyone by hearing from them, or to hear positive feedback about a given option your family is deliberating about.

The hot potato huddle is useful at the beginning of a gathering to set the tone for the rest of the gathering time. Everyone hears from everyone else and all are now able to quickly know what is going on for the family. This tool is also helpful for planning purposes as you look ahead at your week. Knowing that you have a business trip out of town from Wednesday through Friday, the family may need to adapt and schedule around it. Knowing your daughter Sally has her youth soccer end-of-season celebration on Saturday night, the rest of you can plan accordingly. You might be surprised both how much you can say in one minute and how quickly you can go around the table. You will want to allocate as much time in minutes as there are family members present.

2. Deep Huddle

This is a deeper way to check-in with each other.[83] This tool works best with ages ten and up. Using this process, your family will intentionally receive, affirm, and value each person. As each member shares, listen for how God may be speaking through what they say. Estimate the time needed by multiplying the number of family members present by three to five minutes. You can use this process any time you want to build intimacy or deepen your communication and commitment.

- Tell how much time is set aside for the check-in process.
- Choose from among you a facilitator
- Mention the question you will be sharing about. It could be a check-in question such as, "What is going on

in (your name) heart right now?"

Other possibilities:

- A Bible story sharing question such as, "What jumps out at you as you hear this Bible passage?"
- "What is your first reaction to this issue, concern, or opportunity?"
- What positives do you see about this particular option?

- Introduce the check-in process. For example: "To be sure everyone has a chance to talk, this is what we're going to do:

  After we sit quietly for a time, I'll talk first. After I've spoken, I'll invite someone else to talk who may be sitting anywhere in our circle. Before we each speak, or pass, we'll sit quietly for a short time. After the next person has talked, that person gets to invite another to share. If you are not ready to share yet, say, "I pass for now" and then invite someone else. You will be invited again later. If you don't want to say anything at all, simply say "pass" and invite someone else to talk. We will do this until everyone has been invited. If a person "passes for now," we will invite them a second time before ending the check-in process.

  If someone has already said what you want to say, please go ahead and say your thoughts in your own words because it helps your family get a sense of everyone's perspective."

By ensuring that each person has the privilege to invite, the group affirms and values that person. When this process is used for the first time it may feel awkward. You may feel inclined to give up using the deep huddle. While it may at first seem controlling or contrived, with persistence, you will become familiar with this check-in process and will experience its benefits. If a person does not remember to invite the next person, do not invite for him or her. Point out that this person gets to invite the next person to speak. This is especially important when a person passes.

3. Highs and Lows

I stumbled on this tool, trying it with leadership groups. This tool provides permission to explore the highs and the lows of the day, week, or month. St. Ignatius, a 16th century spiritual director, began his classic book ***The Spiritual Exercises*** by suggesting this tool, which he felt was the most important of his exercises.[84] For this tool, allow one to two minutes for each person present.

This tool proclaims the power of God within us as we celebrate cooperating with God with joy. We courageously speak out our experience of separation from God. God is so good and powerful that we can boldly declare the worst of our day without having to uphold some image of ourselves as perfect. It is not our perfection but God's that allows us to remain forever in God's family. We also courageously identify those moments when we felt in unity with God, again, because God is so good and powerful. This tool keeps a profound perspective within you and your family for the unconditional love, goodness, and power of God among you.

In addition, using this tool you may find yourself tuning in more during the day to how you are participating or not participating with God. You become more aware of the nuances of participation with God in God's movement for the world. You are exploring, "*What is it like for me to experience the presence of God?*" You become more present with each other and God.

Using this tool, we are invited to identify moments at the end of a gathering, event, or day or week, where you felt most open and connected toward God's presence and love and when we were most closed, forgetful, or disconnected. Ask God to bring to your heart an awareness of one or two moments or experiences for which you are not grateful, perhaps where you felt anger, sadness, or guilt. Do the same for moments or experiences for which you are grateful.

The process involves quieting yourself as much as you are able and prayerfully exploring and asking two questions:

- For what moment am I most grateful? For what moment am I least grateful?

Other ways to ask the same pair of questions include:

- When did I give and receive the most love today? When did I give and receive the least love today?
- When did I feel most alive today? When did I most feel life draining out of me today?
- When today did I have the most sense of belonging to myself, others, and God? When did I have the least sense of belonging?
- When was I happiest today? When was I saddest?
- What was today's high point? What was today's low point?
- In what moment did my family seem most alive? In what moment did my family seem least alive?
- When did my family give and receive the most love? When did my family give and receive the least love?

Let your creativity have free reign and use what works best for your family. You can use the deep huddle tool as a way to take turns sharing your answers to the two questions. Or, you can simply go around the room, taking turns sharing your highs and lows. Be sure to receive each member non-judgmentally. Do not interrupt their sharing except to ask clarifying questions. Be in nurturing mode, receiving each other as you share.

Over time you may see a pattern of being aligned with God's love and movement for the world. Other times you may see how you are in some way blinded or absorbed in your own wounds or difficulty.

4. Story-Telling

This tool is a way for family members to share successes and failures, an interesting anecdote, a story of someone being transformed by God, or of God at work in your lives, or in your day or week. This tool can encourage your family's efforts in re-imagining and re-telling the family's story in a new context of its vision and journey with God.

Allow plenty of time. You may want to choose a facilitator to guide family members in adhering to a three to five minute limit for their story. You may want to limit the number of stories you share in a given week. Not everyone will always have a story to share. Use this tool as a way of encouraging those who have stories to share them.

You may want to invite the use of this tool by asking during a weekly family gathering, "Does anyone have a story from their week's experiences they'd like to share?" You may need to add additional guidelines such as mentioning you are "inviting stories about people's lives being changed, a mistake you made and learned from, a time where you felt as though you were participating with God, were learning more about God, or a story about God's activity during the week. Any story encouraging us on our journey as a family."

Group-tell is another way to use this tool.[85] Have your family group-tell a story or event in the life of your family. Perhaps you went on a mission trip, donated a gift to someone in need who didn't expect you to donate, or did a family project donating your time cleaning up an elementary school alongside the students' families in an impoverished area of the city.

The group-tell can be done by each person giving a small piece of the story, introducing it with the connector, "*and then....*" When one is aware that an aspect of the story is missing, the connecting words can be, "*but before that .....*" The facilitator should start with "*At the beginning....*" Include people, their expectations, reactions, and ongoing impact.

5. Laser Beam

This tool helps you resolve a problem, issue, concern, or address an opportunity. Because the Bible says if two or more followers of Jesus agree about anything they ask for, it will be done by God, you can be more effective focusing with laser focus on one matter at a time.[86]

- Agree on what your laser beam will focus on. It could be a scheduling concern, encouraging or nurturing a member who is struggling, offering suggestions to someone facing a big event, clutter in the house, changing diet or exercise needs, poor school grades, the use of foul or objectionable language, a road-block in planning for a neighborhood outreach block party.

  Laser beam can be used for just about anything you want to sensitively and effectively address as a family. As problems occur, suggest they be put on the weekly family gathering agenda. If you are a parent, ask for help in solving your problem. Before proceeding, state the proposed subject or focus of the laser beam and then check with every member as to their agreement about the focus of the laser beam. Adapt the proposed focus as needed until you have reached agreement.

Example: A working mother would arrive home each day only to find the house a mess. The kids had left cookie crumbs on and under the table and empty milk glasses. Toys, papers, shoes, socks, and backpacks were everywhere. The mom would start nagging and pleading, "Can you please pick up your things and clean up your messes? You know it upsets me. I love being with you but I lose sight of the joy when I come home to the mess." The children might pick up their things but the mom felt lingering upset and displeasure with the kids and herself.

At the weekly family gathering, the mother admitted this was her problem. It didn't seem to bother the children to have the home cluttered, but she asked if they would be willing to help her find a solution to her problem. The kids, rather than feeling guilt or blame, set about creatively resolving the problem.[87]

- **Begin your laser beam time with prayer.** Ask God for wisdom in addressing the issue and soften your hearts and sharpen your minds to be open to new ideas or ways of resolving the matter.
- **Each person must let go.** Each person must become indifferent to all but what God wants. Being indifferent does not mean you do not care. Rather it means you are open and focused above all on what God wants for this situation, time, and need.
- **Choose your process for discussion.** You can use the brainstorming process described for tuning in your mission message outlined on page 136, the hot potato huddle, the deep huddle, or simply engage in unstructured discussion. You can use the hot potato huddle followed by the deep huddle. You can use a good-on-good review of the positives of each option. You can review and list pros and cons for each option. Simply decide which method or methods to use and stick with it. Again, check in with each member for

their agreement on the proposed process. If you have children, as much as possible stay out of the way and let the children create the solution.

Example: The children came up with a plan for a "safe-deposit box." This was to be a big cardboard box placed in the garage. Anything left out in the common rooms could be picked up by anyone and put in the safe-deposit box. Items would stay one week in the box before the owner could claim it.[88]

- **Make your decision.** If you are using laser beam to encourage, nurture, or coach, rather than to find a solution, then you can simply be in nurturing mode.

6. Vision Mapping

Consider this your vision for your family. It serves as the pathway guide for your journey. Your vision map represents your at-a-glance pathway for how you will achieve your mission.[89] It will be highly visual and no more than one page long. The time outlook for your vision map is two to six months. **The key question is, "*If we are to fulfill our family mission, what vision and goals do we need to pursue in the next two to six months?*"** Ask God for wisdom in deciding what vision and goals to pursue.

You have a mission message defining the essence of your family's mission. Now, you are developing a vision map representing your vision, goals and pathway toward achieving your mission. To tune in your vision map you must answer two questions.

1) What is our main focus right now?
2) How will we gather to discuss and make decisions on our main focus?

What is our main focus?

You must decide what will be your main focus during the next two to six months. This can be your mission message itself (see Figures 4 and 6), a short-term vision that focuses on one aspect of your mission message that you want to strengthen (see Figures 5 and 7), or one of the aspects of a thriving family (nurture, faith, growth, or mission), or some other agreed-upon focus for the next two to six months. Without a main focus, everything becomes important and life becomes overwhelming. We react to whatever may present itself as stressfully important that day. Declaring a main focus defines a pathway for your journey the next two to six months.

You decide the time frame for your map, anywhere between two and six months, and create a vision map for that time frame. As you near the end of that time frame, create a new vision map representing your new main focus for the two to six months after your initial map period. Your new main focus can be the same or a different one.

Vision: This is your short-term rallying cry for advancing your mission message for the next two to six months (see Fig. 5 and 7)). It focuses on one aspect of your mission message that you want to strengthen. This vision establishes a focused, short-term, passionate commitment that best furthers your family's mission, given where you are now on your journey. Your vision goals become your plan for how you will achieve and live out your short-term vision.

If, instead of having a vision focusing on one aspect of your mission message, you choose to focus on your mission message as a whole, then your mission message becomes your vision and your mission goals become your plan for how you will achieve and live out your mission. These goals may be principles that flesh out your mission message. For example, see Example 6 on page 131 in the mission message section above. Four principles expressed within the mission message are (referring to Jesus): loving him, learning from him, loving like him, and, leading like him.

> **Here's an example of a vision:** *Sally and Joe are married with two small children. Joe has a stable, well-paying job but they have more debt than they're comfortable with. Their mission message is "following Jesus for the world." However, they believe that if they can establish a plan for eliminating their debt then they will be more free to follow Jesus for the benefit of the world. Therefore, they decide to make their vision for the next six months, "Stewarding our finances" and include among their vision goals to establish a budget, take a biblical money management course, teach their children about money, and create a high-yield savings account.*

> **Here's an example of a mission message serving as a vision:** *Bridget and James are a young couple who recently began following Jesus, individually and as a couple. Their mission message is, "With Jesus, we donate love to our friends." Because they are new to following Jesus, they decide to focus on their mission message rather than on an aspect of it. They choose to have their mission message be their vision for the next six months: "With Jesus, we donate love to our friends."*

How will we gather to discuss our vision?

Critical to living out your vision is talking about your vision at family gatherings. The Bible says, talk about God's messages in the Bible when you are at home, when you are away on a journey, when you lie down, and when you get up again.[91] You must decide how you will talk about, advance, and make decisions about your top focus during the next two to six months. Many make the effort to live intentionally but fail to generate meaningful change because they do not continue to engage with, measure progress on, act upon, and re-tell their God-guided re-imagined future. Using your vision map encourages you to live out your vision. Your vision map explains the practical meaning and implications of your vision over a two to six month period.

You may find this tool works best used quarterly or every six months. This can be a key strategic tool for your family's journey. Using this tool, you can dynamically engage in the journey of living out your vision. Below is a suggested outline of a process for vision mapping. Whatever process you use, let it serve the purpose of including and valuing every member and assessing and celebrating your progress on your journey. In using the vision map, agree on what to talk about, what issue to decide, allow open debate, and make a decision.

Highs and Lows. Open with either this tool (see pages 173-175) or Story-Telling (see pages 175-176), or both. Allow one to two minutes for each person present. Quiet yourself and prayerfully explore and ask two sets of two questions (feel free to adapt to suit your needs):

- In what moment did I feel most connected with our vision and with God? In what moment did I feel least connected with our vision and God?
- When was my family most in tune with its vision? When was my family least in tune with its vision?

Go around the circle, letting each family member share. Do not interrupt except to ask clarifying questions.

Assess Your Progress. Review your updated vision map progress. If you haven't recently colored in the circles beneath each box on the vision map then do so now. Allow each member to make their own assessment. Do a hot potato huddle reviewing each person's assessments. Then come to agreement on whether to use red, yellow, or green as your family's assessment. Provide everyone an updated colored vision map.

Our Family Vision Map

1. What is our main focus right now?

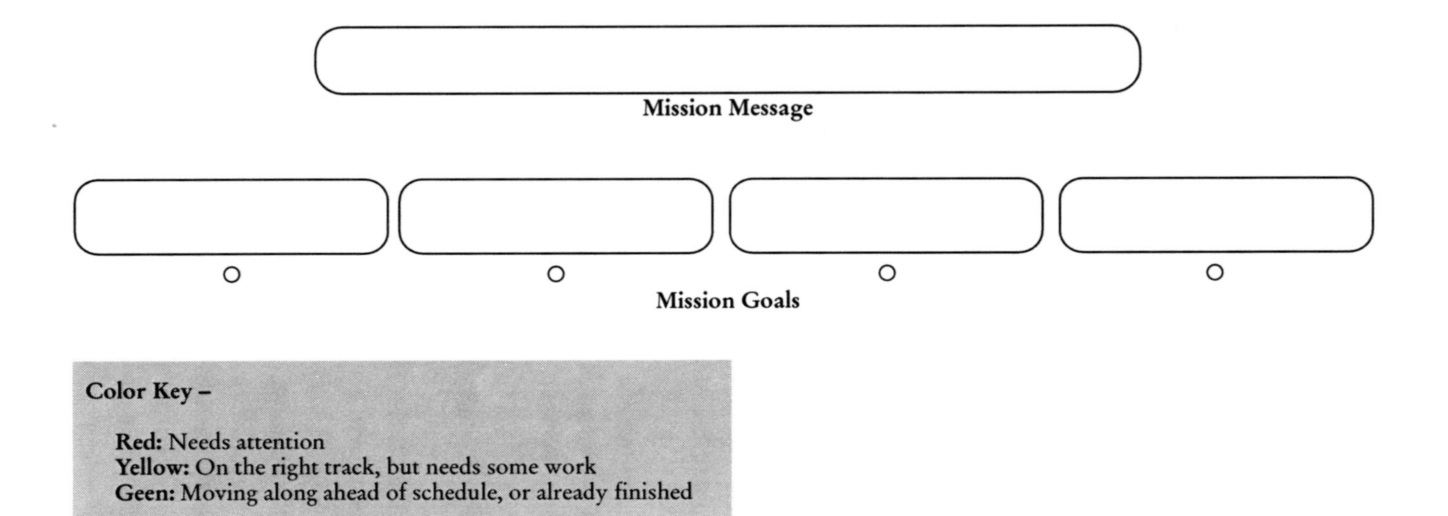

Color Key –

Red: Needs attention
Yellow: On the right track, but needs some work
Geen: Moving along ahead of schedule, or already finished

2. How will we gather to discuss and make decisions about our main focus?

Fig. 4

Our Family Vision Map

1. What is our main focus right now?

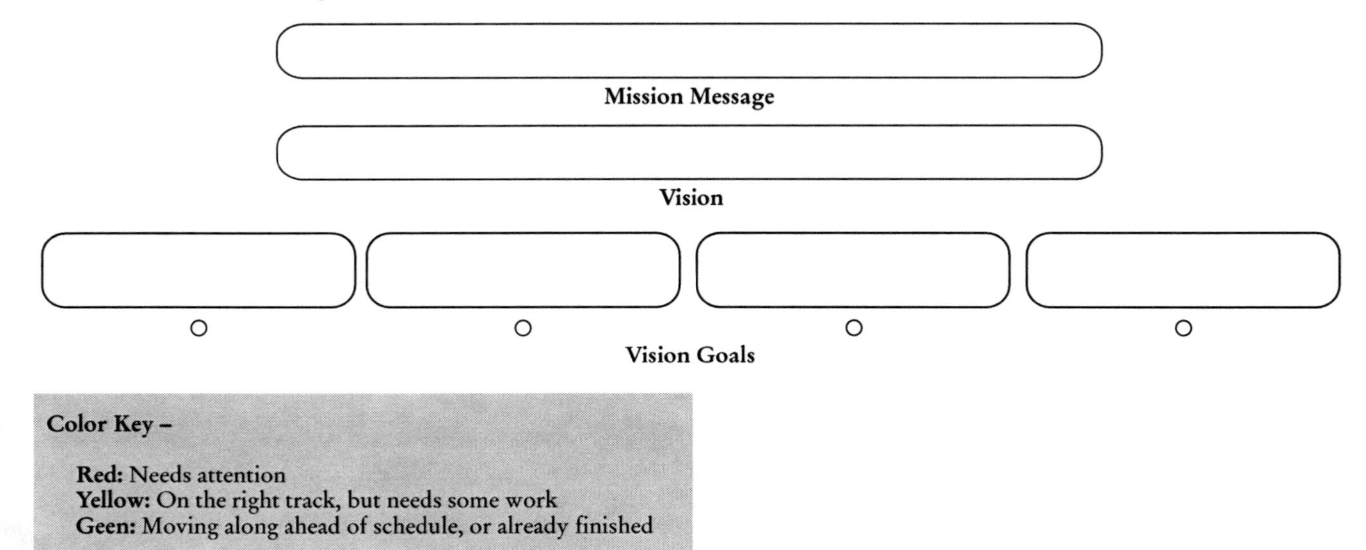

Color Key –

Red: Needs attention
Yellow: On the right track, but needs some work
Geen: Moving along ahead of schedule, or already finished

2. How will we gather to discuss and make decisions about our main focus?

Fig. 5

Our Family Vision Map

1. What is our main focus right now?

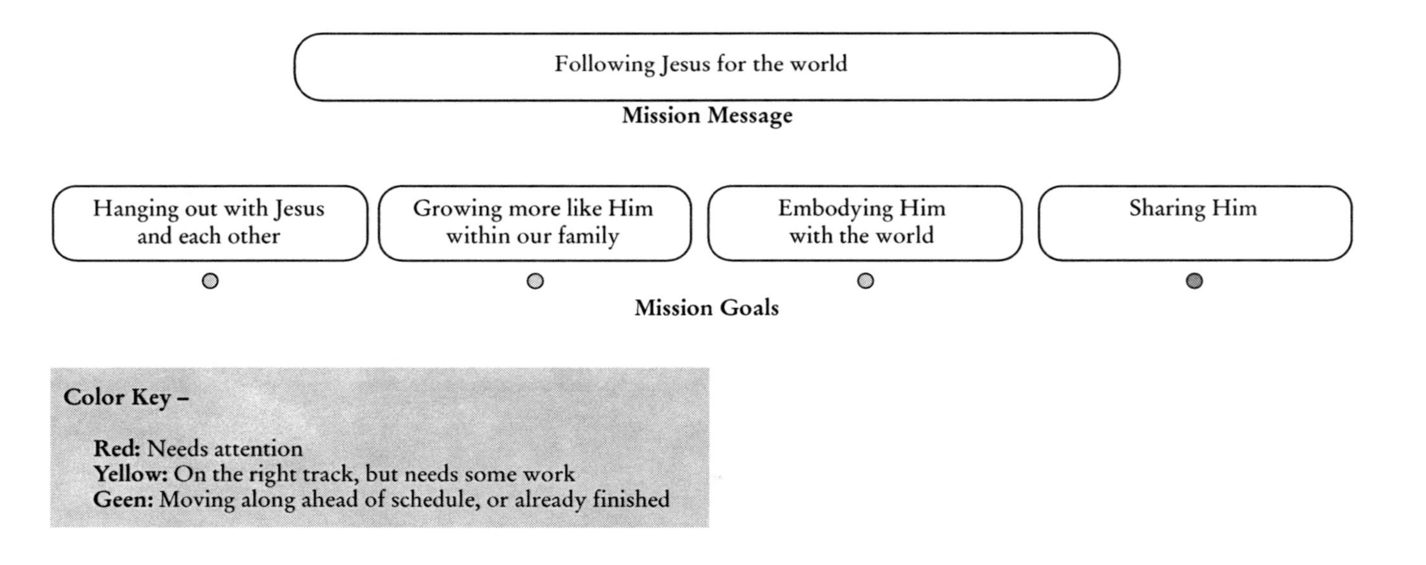

Color Key –

Red: Needs attention
Yellow: On the right track, but needs some work
Geen: Moving along ahead of schedule, or already finished

2. How will we gather to discuss and make decisions about our main focus?

At end-of-month family gatherings.

Fig. 6

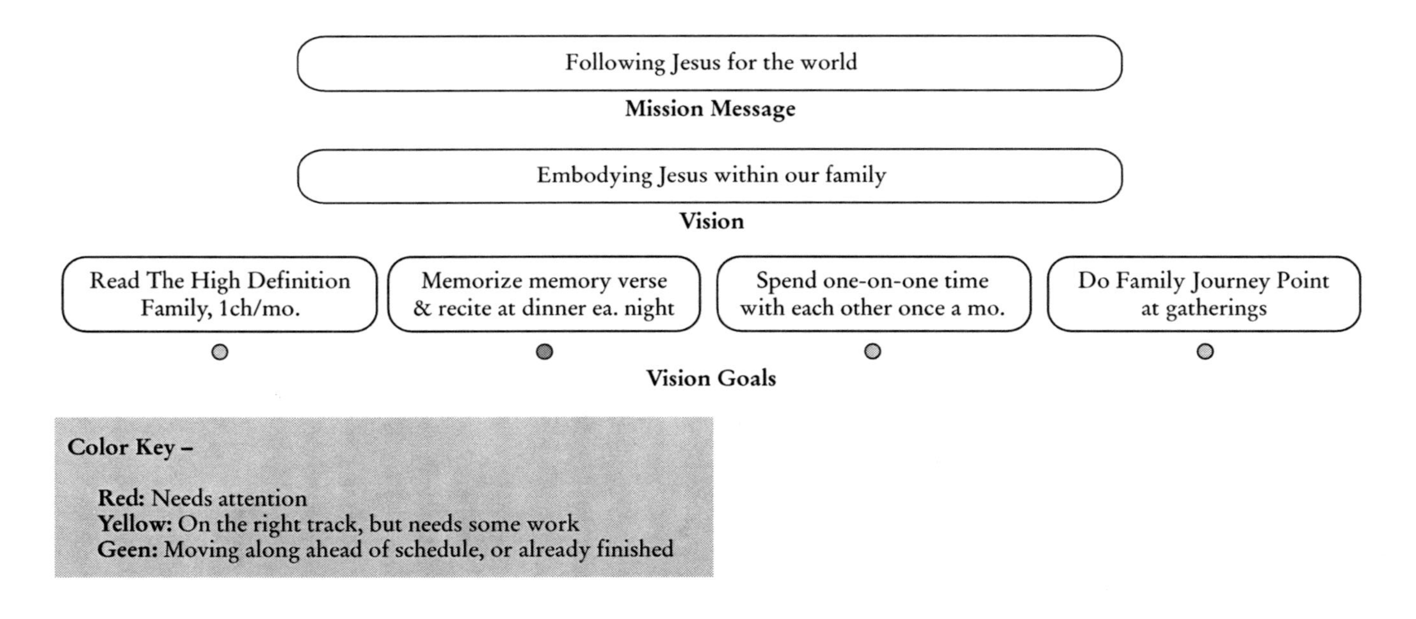

2. How will we gather to discuss and make decisions about our main focus?

While driving to grandparents' house once every three months.

Fig. 7

Set Your Agenda. After you have assessed your progress (and not before) figure out your focus for this vision mapping session. Your focus should become clear as you reflect on and assess your journey.

The possibilities include:
1) Continue with the same vision and goals; 2) Adapt or change the vision and goals based on your assessment; 3) Change your mission message and choose your vision and goals for accomplishing your new mission message; 4) In combination with any of the above, adapting or maintaining how you will gather for vision mapping and making decisions about your main focus.

Discussing and Debating. With your chosen focus in mind, discuss the areas that need improvement and brainstorm possible steps to take to improve those areas.

Encourage and celebrate lively debate. Remember, these are debates about ideas, not personal debates. Do not get your ideas caught up with your ego. Put your ideas out onto the table and let the family do with them what they will. Vigorously advocate for your ideas and easily let go of them when debate is done.

Deciding. Decide on your new vision, goals, and how you will gather for vision mapping. Publish a new vision map —put it on the refrigerator, provide each a copy, or put it on the bathroom mirrors or a kitchen cabinet door! But get it out there so everyone sees the latest map of your family journey!

7. Planning

The focus of this tool is on making preparations and coordinating together an event, day, trip, project, or party. The family simply moves into managing mode with perhaps nurturing and enjoying being secondary modes in using this tool. You function as a team making preparations and plans. **The basis for every decision you make in planning is your vision.** Be sure to move forward as a team with every member on the same page as you make critical planning decisions.

8. Playing

This tool is all about having fun, laughing, even being silly, and experiencing joy together. Instead of always being about improving or growing or becoming more mature, letting loose in play can relieve stress, build relationships, and benefit the family's journey. The key to this tool is not so much in what you do as in simply deciding to focus gathering time on playing. You could go to a baseball game together, or play any kind of game inside or out. Be sure in using this tool to favor a team-oriented approach more than a competitive approach, being encouraging rather than cut-throat.

As an example, if you play Frisbee® golf, form one big Frisbee golf team instead of having everyone compete against each other. You can take turns being the golfer while the others talk strategy, cheer, and encourage the one throwing the Frisbee. Or, if everyone is relatively evenly matched, you can have everyone tee off, select the best shot and have everyone take the next shot from that point, select the best second shot, and so on, until you finish the hole.

If you do engage in a competitive game, be sure everyone is either relatively evenly matched or is mature enough to be humble in victory and constructive in loss, ever encouraging each other on the journey. Charades, floor wrestling, miniature golf, creative team exercises, and Scrabble® have been favorites for us. There are tons of other ways to play. You can even create your own game on the spot.

9. Healing Play

Using this tool can be powerful. This tool can transform the mood, emotions, and energy within your family in the span of just one hour. See the story in chapter fourteen about our children and family being transformed by our choice to engage in healing play, drawing on paper with crayons at the family table. See also the story above about Briana and Caleb and Joe and Kristin. Both of these stories are examples of healing play.

Healing play heals us from old patterns of behavior. We are invited into a new creative cooperative space for seeing and experiencing each other differently, apart from the regular pressures of the day. In healing play, you create an expansive timeless environment drawing out the best within us, nurturing intimate trusting relationships, and creatively addressing challenging obstacles together.

Especially for families with younger children, this tool can be as simple as spreading crayons and paper on the table and slowing down with each other. Even if you only have 30 minutes, pretend you have 30 hours. Slow down. Engage each other. Listen to each other. Give each other the gift of understanding where you actively listen and repeat back to the other a paraphrase of what their needs, feelings, perceptions, or desires are. The crayons and paper become the excuse to slow down and listen to each other. Affirm and value each other.

Healing play can be any kind of team activity, indoors or outdoors. Other examples of healing play: anything resembling a ropes-course-like activity together (see story above); team miniature golf indoors or outdoors; team Frisbee golf; doing a puzzle together; cooking a special dessert together where you are NOT pressed for time; a camping trip; a day-hike with each member taking on responsibilities such as getting snacks together, planning where to hike, and how far; bike riding together. When creating healing play, you want activities cultivating deep communication, cooperation, trust-building, creativity, teamwork, affirmation, and achievement.

10. Learning

This tool can be lots of fun and empowering for every family member. Select who will make a learning presentation at a gathering. The presenters prepare for their presentation by studying, researching, or organizing information, and practicing their presentation. Then, the presenters make their presentation. Think of their presentation as a learning session for everyone involved. The presenters are coaches guiding the others in learning.

We learn best when we know we are responsible for sharing the material with others. This tool encourages and empowers the presenters as they learn by preparing to teach and coach. This tool encourages and empowers the rest of the family as they have an opportunity to learn together. Even when the presenter is a younger child sharing about a particular font of writing style they are using to learn to write, the others can learn as well. When children are the presenters they are thrust into a new role relative to their parents and any older siblings: teacher or coach. Parents get to play the role of student learning from the child. This role reversal is healthy for the development of the child and family relationships.

Whoever is presenting must present in such a way as to engage every member at their level. This tool cultivates an empowering learning culture within the family. Family members are encouraged to engage their curiosity, world, and base of knowledge and experience. Members are encouraged to see themselves as encouragers of one another on the journey.

You could have learning sessions directly related to your vision, such as exploring more about the needs of your neighborhood or community, or of a community in need. You could explore chapter by chapter through a book that helps you learn and use new behavior skills for creating love within your family and circles of influence. The sky is the limit. Use your creativity with what you explore together in learning.

11. Donating Love

This tool may be applied either within your family or in an activity focused on donating to others. Applied within your family, this tool is about intentionally expressing affirmation or unconditionally showering appreciation and love upon one or all of the members of your family.

As an example, you could you could use the deep huddle process for sharing affirmation for another member of your family until all have shared an affirmation. If you do this, let one rule be "no 'buts' included. As in, "You are a great cook but you always seem distracted from cooking well." Another method is to draw names from a hat and express an affirmation to that member.

You could surprise one of your members by each giving this person a small gift expressing your love. The gift could be a massage, a wrapped present, brushing someone's hair, making breakfast, or washing their car.

You can also apply this tool with neighbors, friends, acquaintances, or strangers. When you go on a mission trip, donating love is the gathering tool you are using. Your family can decide on a project, spontaneously or planned, that will benefit others. It could be washing a neighbor's car or raking their leaves, shoveling their snow, cleaning a widow's attic or garage, putting up Christmas lights for an older neighbor, watching your neighbor's kids while their parents go out on a date. You could drop a gift basket at the front door of your neighbors (*ring the doorbell and run!?*). Use your creativity and pass along the love you receive from your leader.

12. Worshiping

This tool may be used alongside other tools and activities at a gathering or as a stand-alone time of devotion with your family worshiping God. This does not need to be complicated or formal. You are the creators of your worship time. You can be formal, informal, light candles or not and sing songs or not. You can create a special worship space. We use a small card table designed for children to play at. We often set out a napkin spread out to function as a table cloth. Depending on your own faith tradition, doctrine, and practices, you could serve the Jesus meal or set out an empty cup and a plate with bread on it to remind you of Jesus' sacrifice upon the cross for us.

Whatever you do, create the space so that you can best worship and focus on God. The basic idea of worship is to gratefully gather, celebrate who God is, receive from God nourishment for the journey, then to go out and serve others empowered by God. You can spend your whole time praising God, or for families with younger children—essentially saying, "*Yeah, God!*" You can spend time praying, singing, reading from the Bible, offering back to God, and going out in commitment with God for the benefit of the world.

In offering back to God you could write on a piece of paper what you are grateful for or you could offer your updated vision map and burn that in the fireplace as an offering of gratitude to God for what God is doing through you. You could place money in an offering plate and give this to your church as your tithe. Use your imagination.

In going out in commitment you could each recite your vision, or say something like, "*Bless you O God as we go as a member of your forever family, moving with you for the world!*"

You can use musical instruments. You can read a passage and invite each to share what jumps out at them from the passage. You could pause with a moment of silence between each person's sharing. Use your imagination and enjoy and worship God. This tool supplements and encourages your relationship and worship experience with your church.

Other Tools for Other Gatherings:

Hurricane

This tool, especially for families with younger children, is essential for sanity! You declare a hurricane and everyone in the house immediately joins as a team cleaning up the house. This tool is useful if you suddenly are confronted with a messy house and an opportunity to host someone's visit with you. We use this tool on a nearly daily basis.[90]

No one has to bear the responsibility alone for a sometimes drudgerous task. By choosing this tool, cleaning up becomes fun, easier, and a team-building exercise.

Yearly Review

This tool is intended for taking a step back and looking at how you are doing as a family on your journey. Think of this as a yearly vision mapping exercise. Topics you might cover at a yearly review are:

- **Strategic Visioning Review:** Take a look at your family's vision map: its mission message, vision, and goals. The key questions are, "*Are our vision and goals the wisest for achieving our vision? Is our mission message the wisest choice for our family right now?*"
- **Faith Aspect Review:** The key question is, "*Are our family members growing in their relationship with Jesus?*"
- **Nurturing Aspect Review:** Ask yourself, "*Does our family provide an environment most nurturing of each member?*" If not, what can we do differently to make ourselves and our family be more nurturing?
- **Personal Growth Aspect Review:** The key question is, "*Is each member growing more in character like Jesus?*"
- **Mission Aspect Review:** The key question is, "*Are we as a family moving with God for the world as well as we could be? If not, what can we do differently?*"

After you have reviewed your vision and made any changes, be sure to consciously commit together to your vision for the year ahead.

Family Journey Point: Chapter Fifteen

To Ponder: When I imagine our family gathering using some of the tools described in this chapter, I see us...

To Consider: Commit to gathering together often to encourage each other in living out your family vision.

To Remember: *"I want us to help each other with the faith we have. Your faith will help me, and my faith will help you"*

Romans 1:25 (NCV)

One-On-One Relationships

16

Friends love through all kinds of weather, and families stick together in all kinds of trouble.

Proverbs 17:17 (MSG)

"How can I nurture my relationship with each family member?"

Our sixth anniversary was approaching. We had six-month old twin boys and a three-year-old daughter. We hadn't been out much as a couple. Good friends of ours volunteered to come and watch our kids while we went out to celebrate. With all the diaper-changing, nursing, feeding, and care of our kids, our relationship as a couple had taken a big back seat. We went out to dine at a Mexican restaurant down the street and had a grand time. In just an hour and a half, we rediscovered ourselves as husband and wife and were rejuvenated.

Relationships are at the core of following Jesus as a family. Besides your relationship with Jesus, your relationship with each other is critical to your journey. You have lots of friends but only one biological family. Enjoy nurturing your relationship with each of your siblings, if you have any, and parents, grandparents, uncles, aunts, and cousins. These relationships are the fabric of your story being woven together with God's story through your vision.

Accepting Each Other Perfectly

Because God is the leader of your family, you choose to look at life through the lens of Jesus' unconditional love. You choose to accept that you are accepted by God. You also choose to accept others just as you are accepted by God.[91] Because you accept both yourself and others unconditionally, you are most able to love through all kinds of circumstances and difficulties. Whatever the circumstance, you accept them.

You recognize we all face an infinite number of choices every day shaping our attitudes, health, character, and who we are as people. We don't always make good choices. Yet, you know and claim your own acceptance by God. You know and claim others' acceptance by God. And, you accept them.

Being Loyal to Each Other

When you accept others perfectly you are perfectly loyal to them, both when they are present and when they are not. You speak about others when they are not present as though they were and in a way that accepts and honors them. When you speak this way about your family members you build each other up and nurture the beauty of your family culture.

When you hear someone else talking about a family member who is not present, in a way that would not be spoken were the person present, then you have three common responses. You can leave. You can ignore the comments and not pass them along. You can interrupt the person and ask that they stop making the comments.

If you leave, the person talks on and you are left uncomfortably enabling the person's behavior and the impact it can have on the person being talked about.

If you ignore the comments and let them die with you, you enable the speaker's behavior and ignore the injustice done.

If you interrupt the person, you risk derailing your relationship with the speaker and with any others present by performing the role of whistle-blower. You put yourself in an uncomfortable position of embarrassing the speaker in front of others.

Which action do you choose? Whichever of the three you choose you are faced with less than a win-win situation. However, you have resources for handling conflict and for nurturing the one-on-one relationships in your family.

An alternative to consider: Interrupt the person speaking and calmly and matter-of-factly say, "Jill, I'm feeling uncomfortable with how we are talking about (so-and-so). I'd like instead to talk about …."

You've made the effort necessary to stop the person from continuing to speak hurtfully—that's in line with God's character. You acknowledge being a party to the harmful conversation, even as listener, where you are joined with the person speaking the offense of talking about your family member in a disloyal way. You have said you are "feeling uncomfortable with how *we* are talking about (so and so) …"—and that is in line with God's character. You've indicated a desire to continue talking, accepting a continuing relationship with the speaker and the others—that's in line with God's character. And, you participate with God in nurturing one-on-one relationships in your family.

Recognizing One-on-One Time as Essential

What if everyone in your family affirmed the value of spending time one-on-one with each other? What if, whether taking time to go on a date or down to the hardware store, you were intentional about spending time one-on-one. What if you aimed to do what the other would enjoy? You might prefer an action film but your daughter prefers a chick-flick. You might prefer to go out to dinner but your spouse prefers to go for a hike. You might prefer hitting golf balls on the driving range but your son prefers going to the baseball batting cage. What if you chose an outing that best encourages interaction between you? I myself prefer meals to movies, as much as I enjoy movies, for that reason.

Whether you are a couple with no children at home or are parents with children at home, be sure to go out on regular dates. You may want to decide how often is often enough. Once a month or so? Once a week? Once every couple of months? Going out somehow rekindles your relationship as a couple. Going out consciously says to yourselves, and perhaps others, you are a couple! Going out gives you the opportunity to talk and relate as a couple and not house mates or parents, though those you may also be.

Relying on the One Perfect Relationship You Have

You may adore your loved ones, enjoy being with them, being blood family with them, and on a journey with them. Yet, if you examine your relationships carefully, you understand your loved ones don't always hold up their end of the bargain.

Maybe your loved ones have been late for dinner, have forgotten your birthday, regretfully spoken a word of harmful anger, expressed an arrogant attitude toward another person or people, have behaved defensively or hurtfully in conflict, have not always done what was right. Perhaps they behaved nicely when behaving truthfully would have been more direct and loving with you. Maybe they gave advice when a suggestion would have been more empowering of you. Perhaps they passively kept silent when they could have asserted their legitimate needs. Or perhaps they have told little white lies. If you expect your relationship with your loved ones will be perfect, you will be disappointed again and again. I expect you have already discovered this and have experienced disappointment. Yet you call your loved one *loved* precisely because you love them still.

Before you and I become too comfortable in assessing our disappointment of our loved ones, understand we too must be joined with them as members of a group called humanity, whose harm and hurts have caused others pain. If you are parents, you want to be perfect for your kids. *But you can't—you're not God.*

The good news is you can enjoy a perfect relationship with someone who commits no errors, mistakes, fudging, or slights, and has no shortcomings, gray areas, conditional acceptance, or misunderstandings in their behavior toward you. No, I am not a matchmaking guru setting you up with the perfect mate. But consider this–what if you were to ever more rely upon and nurture your relationship with God, who never lets you down?[92] You might have expectations unfulfilled by God but God comes through one hundred percent of the time on God's promises and love for you. You need perfection in at least one relationship—yours with God. *And God delivers.* You are not perfect but God is. And you with your warts and all become perfectly intertwined with God, all because God is perfect and perfectly loves you.

The icing on the cake of this perfect relationship is while God perfectly accepts you just as you are, God loves you too much to leave you unchanged. God leads you instead on a journey, providing you everything you need to shape your character, here a little, there a little, more and more into the character of your leader.

Seeing Yourselves as an Organic Team

As you follow Jesus, your family is alive! You are filled with all of what you need to be everything you were intended to be. The Bible refers to followers of Jesus as being like the human body, interconnected, altogether one.[93] You live, breathe, move, and interact, as one body or team. Yet when we sit and read a book, say, we primarily call into action our eyes for reading, our hands for holding the book, and our mind for engaging the story. Our legs, torso, and hair are not being actively engaged.

In the same way, for families with three members or more, engaging every smaller combination of groupings possible in activities and relationship-building makes more dynamic your family as a whole. For example, feeling free as a family of four going on an outing to the farmers' market with two or three of you encourages a stronger dynamic, a stronger identity, for your family as a whole.

Be sure every member is an equal active teammate on your family's journey. When you have family gatherings engage your whole family. Always have every member's best interests at heart. Yet, if everyone knows you have a regularly occurring scheduled gathering then you could consistently hold the gathering whether everyone is present or not. You don't want one family member's busy schedule, forgetfulness, or irresponsible behavior to cause your family journey to come to a screeching halt.

My toddler sons argued over who should receive the last hard-boiled egg. Their argument escalated. I stepped between their lunch chairs at the table, knelt to their level and said, "Guys," pausing to get their attention, "You are on the same team. What team are you on?"

"The Strauch team!" they said.

"Okay, so you're on the Strauch team. Because you're on the same team, you look after each other. With one hard-boiled egg left, what can you do?"

They sat waiting for me to provide the answer.

"What if you share the egg? Did you know that God made the eggs and God makes lots of eggs. In fact, there's more in the refrigerator. You can share the cooked egg and I can cook more. You can have another half-egg in half an hour. What do you think?"

They nodded vigorously in agreement.

You are growing together as a dynamic team whose story is daily being woven into the story and movement of God for the world.

Family Journey Point: Chapter Sixteen

To Ponder: Are there ways that I can spend one-on-one fun time with each member of the family?

To Consider: Because God lives inside of you, you have what it takes to accept and nurture each other on your journey together.

To Remember: *"Friend's love through all kinds of weather, and families stick together in all kinds of trouble."*

Proverbs 17:17 (MSG)

Family Leadership

But among you it will be different. Whoever wants to be a leader among you must be your servant, and whoever wants to be first among you must become your slave.

17

Matthew 20:26-27 (NLT)

"How can I encourage leadership if we're supposed to be 'followers?"

I was fifteen. I walked up the driveway and spotted our large garbage bin in the driveway and continued right on past it into the house. The next day I again saw the garbage bin in the same spot and moved right on past it into the house. The third day, the bin remained. Again, I walked inside. So did my older sisters and my nine-year-old brother.

As we were finishing dinner on the third day our father calmly but with his voice betraying a sense of disgust and disappointment said, "Have you guys seen the garbage bin outside in the driveway?"

"Yes, it's been out there at least a couple days now," I replied, now feeling guilty of neglect and poor judgment.

Our dad asked, "Why didn't you do anything about it?"

"Because that's something you have usually taken care of," I mustered.

He said, "I purposely left the bin out there to see what would happen."

If we are followers of Jesus how can we be leaders? And what do we mean by "leaders?" Is a leader someone who has all the answers? Someone who has all the power? Is a leader someone who calls all the shots, or at least the important ones? Does the leader decide what others can and cannot do?

Jesus himself says the characteristics, posture, and nature of leadership for followers is different from that for the rest of the world. Jesus says if we are to become leaders we must become servants of all. He turns upside down the competitive, power-holding, authority-wielding way of leadership. For Jesus, leadership is wholly different. Jesus himself is the ultimate leader and demonstrates the kind of leadership he talks about. Notice how he is also the ultimate follower of God, continually seeking out and relating with God on his journey to the cross. Note especially his prayer, "*Father, not what I want but let what you want be done....*"[94]

In the tension between being both a follower and a leader, we must understand what Jesus means by following and what he means by leading. Jesus himself embodies this tension. You can be a faithful follower and a powerful leader filled with a power of a different kind and for a different purpose from that used by conventional leaders.

The Bible says that in following Jesus we are to grow up into his character. Jesus says once we know and are aware of God and God's story and love one another as he loves us then we are his friends.[95] Jesus was uniquely a follower of God because he perfectly followed God. We who are followers of God rely upon the unique gift of God in Jesus which sustains us in our imperfection. **It is Jesus' perfection which allows us to be made perfect through him.** Followers learn from Jesus and receive power from Jesus for growing more like him.

The Bible invites us not only to be followers of Jesus but to do as he does and lead others to know and accept God's desire for them to weave their messy story into the story of God and become part of the forever team with God.[96] Jesus' leadership represents not just God's desire for us to be leaders in the unfolding story of God but God's gift to us of all we need to be just that.

Jesus was uniquely a leader as he is worthy of our worship and leading our lives. He pioneered the way in defeating evil and clearing a pathway for our union and journey with God. No one else could have opened this pathway. The center of history occurs in his leadership as he journeys toward the cross, even though he made no mistakes, and takes on all the mistakes and brokenness of the world.[97] John the Baptist, the one who baptized Jesus, said essentially, "*Behold, the lamb of God who takes away the mistakes and brokenness of the world.*"[98]

Fifty-five different times in the Bible Jesus noted in one way or another that he would go to the cross, die upon the cross to wipe clean the slate of your life, and be risen on the third day.[99] Jesus being risen from the dead puts an exclamation mark on Jesus' leadership for our lives. His being risen from the dead means Jesus was who he claimed to be, had the power he claimed to have, and did what he promised he would do. Jesus being risen from the dead means his leadership in your family can transform not only the way you live and die but the way you lead.

As a leader, your power comes from being a follower. You cannot divorce yourself one from the other. The more you surrender to Jesus' leadership as a follower the more you are able to allow God to shape you into the leader you are empowered and made to be. Because you follow Jesus you have the presence of Jesus within you. Jesus' presence is a power inside of you greater than any power outside of you. This power within you continually shapes you more into the image of God and empowers you into greater participation in the unfolding story of God for the world.

This presence and power lives and flows within you like streams of living water and teaches you, guides you, reminds you of everything your leader has said to you, and empowers you to be selflessly pointing to God's way. It shapes you, opens your spiritual eyes, strengthens, comforts, counsels you and intercedes for you. This presence and power is the means by which you are part of the bigger story of God for the world.[100]

Quiet time fuels action time. When you hang out with Jesus you receive the flow of his presence and power within and through you. This presence and power of God within you makes possible your effective leadership. Your leadership is modelled on the character and leadership of Jesus and so seeks to be selfless, far-sighted, compassionate, humble, and powerful. Your leadership seeks always to donate and express unconditional love, and be aligned with what God is doing. You seek ways to cooperate in allowing God to weave and use the messiness of your story and others' into God's own unfolding story for the world.

Jesus is a high definition leader. He sets out a clear vision and purpose for followers. He teaches them the unfolding story of God, consistently behaves in alignment with God's unconditional love for all, and gives followers the freedom and permission to use their creativity, passion, and shape in participating with God. He creates a big open space for his followers to exercise their own leadership for the benefit of others and grow more into the image and character of God.

Tune in your vision and live it out

The Master chose seventy-two others and sent them two by two ahead of him to every town and place where he was about to go. He gave them this charge:

'What a huge harvest! And how few the harvest hands. So on your knees; ask the God of the Harvest to send harvest hands.

On your way! But be careful—this is hazardous work. You're like lambs in a wolf pack. Travel light. Comb and toothbrush and no extra luggage. Don't loiter and make small talk with everyone you meet along the way.

When you enter a home, greet the family, 'Peace.' If your greeting is received, then it's a good place to stay. But if it's not received, take it back and get out. Don't impose yourself.

Stay at one home, taking your meals there, for a worker deserves them. Don't move from house to house, looking for the best cook in town.

When you enter a town and are received, eat what they set before you, heal anyone who is sick, and tell them, 'God's kingdom is right on your doorstep!'

... 'The one who listens to you, listens to me. The one who rejects you, rejects me. And rejecting me is the same as rejecting God, who sent me.'

The seventy-two came back triumphant. 'Master, even the demons danced to your tune!'[101]

Jesus set out a clear vision: *We're the realm of God sent to your doorstep*. He expressed the following beliefs:

- God provides all we need;
- Followers are partners with God in God's unfolding story ("The one who listens to you, listens to me. The one who rejects you, rejects me. And rejecting me is the same as rejecting God, who sent me.")
- Followers are leaders inviting others into the realm of God; ("God's kingdom is right on your doorstep!")
- The unfolding story of God is urgent! ("Don't loiter and make small talk.")

Jesus set out guidelines:

- Don't take a heavy suitcase
- Don't loiter and make small talk
- Don't move from house to house

The clearer your family purpose, the clearer the boundaries within which all sorts of creative gifted participation can occur. The clearer your vision the less chance ambiguity will derail creativity and gifted leadership within your family. The clearer your vision the less chance egos will discourage an environment of creativity, growth, learning, nurture, mission, and leadership. You have a vision for moving forward with God in the midst of the messiness of your story and life. And, like the seventy-two who came back triumphant, you live it out.

Get to know and tell the story of God

Then Jesus came to them and said, 'All authority in heaven and on earth has been given to me. Therefore go and make disciples of all nations, baptizing them in the name of the Father and of the Son and of the Holy Spirit, and teaching them to obey everything I have commanded you. And surely I am with you always, to the very end of the age.'[102]

Being knowledgeable about what the Bible says, who Jesus is, what he has done and is doing prepares you to teach others about the story of God. Your own experience of a deep transformative relationship with Jesus also prepares you to teach others about the unfolding movement of God for the world. Because your story is weaving into God's, telling your own story is a most powerful way of telling God's story.

Telling your story

While your story, if anything like mine, is messy, here are some suggestions or guidelines for sharing. You can apply these guidelines to sharing about your messy family story or about your messy personal story.[103] The examples below are for a family story.

Before Jesus…

Question 1: Where were you spiritually before you began your relationship with Jesus? How did that affect you—your feelings, attitudes, actions, thoughts, and relationships?

Example: *We struggled with fights about money, communicating our expectations, and keeping our tempers in check. We attended church together but we mostly left God at the door. As a result, our kids fought, were disrespectful to each other and us. None of us much relied on God for the struggles we faced. I was an insecure defensive leader of our family.*

Question 2: What caused you to begin considering Jesus for your journey?

Example: *A guest speaker at our church one Sunday explained that most parents try to go it alone in leading their family. He said Jesus is the leader we need for our family. He alone provides our security and purpose for living in alignment with God as a family together.*

Accepting Jesus…
Question 3: What shift happened that made you want to journey with Jesus?

Example: *We had been social followers of Jesus. We had tried immersing ourselves in the kids' sports, their school activities, learning new parenting techniques, and occasional community projects. However, I realized the guest pastor was right. They were not providing me and us security. Only Jesus could do that.*

Question 4: How did you accept Jesus as the leader of your life and forgiver of your soul?

Example: *We talked about how we longed to be part of something bigger than ourselves as a family. We prayed together and shared our brokenness with God. We asked Jesus to forgive us for leaving him out of our family life, messy as it is, and relying upon ourselves. Then we each asked Jesus to come into our lives and our home to lead each of us and our family and give us that security and purpose we had been looking for.*

After Jesus...
Question 5: How did your life begin to change after you trusted Jesus for your journey?

Example: *We no longer felt insecure and fearfully inadequate. We began to feel more confident, whole, and peaceful because we knew God was in control.*

Question 6: What other benefits have you experienced since becoming a follower of Jesus?

Example: *Our parenting improved—we knew we weren't the ultimate leader. We were now accountable right along with the kids in our new journey. We have become focused and excited at the possibilities of our family's growth. We're not as afraid of the messiness of our life. We are telling a new story using the messiness of our old story. We are living our faith, nurturing each other on a new journey. We're actually starting to get creative in how we can donate love away to others.*

Your messy story can lead others with their own messy stories into the bigger story of God for the world. Whenever you learn about or experience God, share what you learn or experience as soon as you can. Not only will you encourage your own learning and experiencing but you will help others get to know the story of God. You will be a witness to God in the midst of others. You can encourage leadership by nurturing and valuing the journey of others.

Model this leadership in your own behavior

As you grow in character more like Jesus your behavior more truly points to Jesus. You demonstrate to your family and others the forever benefits of being a follower of Jesus and a leader with Jesus. Yet modeling after Jesus' character and leadership does not mean you have your act together. Being spiritually mature includes being humble in recognizing the messiness of your family story and life. It means you are a follower who leads as you are led. Being a spiritually mature leader means you rely upon the gift of God in being both a follower and a leader and not upon having your act together. Being more like Jesus in character means you are cooperating in allowing God to weave the messiness of your story and life into the unfolding story of God for the world.

Give family members lots of creative space

You can give family members the freedom and permission to explore and use their creativity, passion, and shape in participating with God. One of the biggest temptations for leaders is to micromanage those they lead. We think if our job is to lead we should make sure others do things the way we would do them. The difficulty with this thinking is our way is not the way. Jesus' leadership did include his saying, "*I am the way and the truth and the life*" precisely because he uniquely *is* the way.[104] Yet, he set out as big a territory as possible within which others could follow and lead.

He gave the seventy-two a vision, "*We're the realm of God sent to your doorstep!*" He gave guidelines serving as a floor boundary: Don't dilly dally, don't pack lots of luggage, and don't go from house to house. Between the vision and the list of "don'ts" was lots of creative space. The followers could decide what to say, who to approach first, who to stay with, and build their own relationships. They had a lot of freedom, a lot of room, from which to be leaders carrying out the vision. The vision created a lot of space because it was clear and big. The guidelines created a lot of space because it was clear and spells out the specifics of what they're not to do.

Those who seek to control others seek to maintain an adult-child relationship. These leaders stifle their families and the lives of those they lead. They inhibit leadership development and set stumbling blocks between others and God. Jesus has very harsh words for those who seek to control the lives and growth of others.

The challenge for parents, especially of younger children, is where to settle on the continuum between necessary parental control and the permission-giving necessary to nurturing creative leadership. However, rather than seeing the choice as being between permissiveness with no limits and excessive control, tuning in your family vision means you have kindness and firmness at the same time. You have freedom with order. Lots of choices are available but within limits showing respect and honor for all. You have a positive and principle-focused discipline.

Taming the Temper Tantrums of Children
"How can I raise my child into a leader?"

I read this anecdote by Charlie Shedd, an author and pastor. He wrote:

> *Before we had kids, I used to travel across the country teaching a lecture I called, "The Ten Commandments for Raising Perfect Kids." After Martha and I had our first child, I changed the title to, "Ten Hints for Parents." After our second child, I renamed my title to, "A Few Tentative Suggestions for Fellow Strugglers." After the arrival of our third child, I gave up speaking on the topic altogether!*[105]

It seems there are as many styles, methods, and ways of raising children as there are parents. Most all of them have pieces of wisdom and truth for parents to apply. However, if you're going to raise a child to explore both following Jesus and becoming a leader as a follower, **I suggest that whatever you do, find a way to involve your child in finding a solution to their trouble.**

The key is in using parenting techniques that align with what Jesus is about. Parenting techniques and behaviors that impart shame, embarrassment, or guilt contribute to the very things Jesus came to overcome. We add baggage and hurdles that our child must overcome in arriving at a place of accepting the total love and acceptance Jesus offers them. We make smaller an already small child who by the gift of God embodies the very temple of the living God. And, we add to our feeling inadequate and frustrated as a parent.

> *Our three-year-old boys are fighting over who gets to sit in a pink recliner chair. I know what you're thinking, "Pink?" What boy would want to sit in a pink chair?! Yet, they're pushing, yelling, and tussling. I come on the scene.*
>
> *Nathan, while continuing to push, says, "I want to sit here too!"*
>
> *"Ian, do you want to share with Nathan right now?," I ask.*
>
> *Ian, pushes back and replies, "I want to sit here by myself!"*
>
> *"Nathan, I have a problem. Ian was sitting in this chair first and doesn't want to share the chair with you right now. He wants to sit in the chair by himself. Do you have any ideas about how we can solve my problem?," I ask.*
>
> *He calms considerably, eases up and slides away from the chair and softly replies, "Yeah." And moves on.*

In times past, I would have used other ways that would have imposed a solution upon them, anything from imposing upon Nathan the choice between backing away or have a time out to settle down (*some choice, huh!*), to playfully cajoling Ian or insisting that he share. Or, I'd insist that Nathan step away and I'd impose a time out if he escalated his resistance to my imposed solution. Nathan would feel small, powerless, guilty, shameful, and embarrassed. He would get the message that in order to make it in this world he would have to become powerful, do the right things, and do them perfectly. Instead, gratefully, he gets the message that he has the power to make choices, including, ultimately, to become both a follower and a leader of Jesus.[106]

Chores and Children
"What about keeping up with chores?"

Chores have a way of having their way in the house. They can overwhelm any sense of sanity, peace, and rest in a busy household. Your family vision orients the task of household chores into the bigger picture of your lives as followers of Jesus and leaders in your family and in the world. Here are a couple of strategies for keeping up with chores and moving forward with your vision.

Chore Visioning

By creating a framework for nurturing each family member's leadership skills, chores go from being dreaded sources of conflict to being another way for encouraging leadership. Chore visioning is a way of providing as much creative space possible for developing leadership skills and initiative. This process works especially well for parents with young children or teens though it also can be used with adults.[107] Here's how chore visioning works.

Chore Message

Establish a short chore message for the chore. The chore message must be very short, memorable, and bring to mind the responsibilities of the chore.

Example: My four-year-old daughter and I agreed she would clean up papers spread all over the floor in her room and organize them into a three-ring binder. This particular example is for a non-repeating chore. I said, "Your mission for this task is '*Clean and Sort.*" The essence of her chore was set clearly in her mind and mine.

Coach

Second, achieve consensus with your child or family member on who their coach will be. Who can they come to for ideas, suggestions, information, or other help?

Example: I asked my daughter if she would be open to me serving as her coach for her *Clean and Sort* project. She agreed.

Guidelines

Third, set out the guidelines for the chore. What should the person *not* do in carrying out this responsibility? You may want to consider including "no illegal activities," "no activities against the HOA guidelines."

Example: No throwing re-usable paper in the trash. No pens. No scissors without supervision.

Huddle Time

Fourth, set out in advance when the coach will meet with the person to see how the chore is going. The coach and the person have an accountability huddle about the progress or lack of progress with the chore. For ongoing chores you may want to set weekly or monthly huddle times.

Example: We agreed to meet before dinner to see how she was doing.

Reward

Decide, perhaps with the child or person, what the reward will be for successfully carrying out the chore vision. Not every chore will lend itself to a tangible reward. The reward for some chores may be a feeling of belonging, something each family member simply does as part of the family. Other chore rewards for children may be specific, an increase in allowance, or in their role in leading a family mission project, or getting their favorite dinner or dessert.

> Example: If you successfully achieve the chore vision of *clean and empty trash* for three weeks then we'll raise your allowance 50 cents and we'll go out for ice cream!

The Laser Beam Revisited

The use of the Laser Beam tool for family gatherings is a powerful way for the family to nurture leadership and problem-solving skills among its members. Parents can avoid many hassles with their children by suggesting that problems be handled with the laser beam approach at a gathering. The keys are:

- Share the problem in a family gathering
- Have children create the solution, as much as possible
- Children enforce the rules and parents stay out of enforcement, as much as possible
- The rules apply to everyone in the family, including parents

Suggest children brainstorm solutions for the problem, not consequences for past behavior. Invite them to brainstorm ideas helpful for the future. See more about brainstorming on page 136.

Involving children in this way eliminates some discipline hassles. The children have opportunities to develop leadership skills and to learn and practice problem-solving skills as a family on a weekly basis. Often, these skills carry on into the week. Children develop esteem and skills in being capable, a contributor, a force of influence, understanding and productively channeling their emotions, working with others and developing friendship, empathy, negotiating, sharing, and listening skills.

They develop the ability to be aware of and interactive within a system, developing flexibility, adaptability, integrity, and understanding both the vision and the limits and consequences of everyday life. They develop an appreciation for and ability to use wisdom and to evaluate options on the basis of a vision, beliefs, and values. They become followers of Jesus and leaders with Jesus.

Family Journey Point: Chapter Seventeen

To Ponder: In what moment during the last week did you feel most powerful? In what moment did you feel least powerful? Was jesus powerful? Share, as you are willing.

To Consider: Commit to being both a follower of Jesus and a leader with Jesus.

To Remember: *"But among you it will be different. Who-ever wants to be a leader among you must be your ser-vant..."*

Romans 12:5 (NIV)

Fine-Tuning Your Vision

18

... You will tell everyone about me in Jerusalem, in all Judea, in Samaria, and everywhere in the world.

Acts 1:8b (CEV)

"Where do we go from here?"

Heidi and I had first tuned in our family vision in October of 2000. We had been married about six months. Friends of ours graciously hosted our stay on their second-floor flat at their retreat house. Heidi and I spent two or three days going through a process of tuning in our family vision. Our family was just us two—one who served as an attorney and the other as a pastor. We slightly modified our vision a time or two but essentially our vision remained the same.

In the span of three years we had three children. We decided one night in November of 2007 it was time we fine-tuned our vision to reflect our new family. Fine-tuned is probably not the word. Re-done is more accurate. The new vision we tuned in needed to be meaningful for our two two-year-old boys and our five-year-old daughter. What was our new vision? "Following Jesus!" Perhaps in a year or two we'll fine-tune to "Following Jesus for the world."

Regularly examine your vision in light of any changes in your family circumstances and in opportunities and circumstances around you calling out for adapting your current journey direction. There is no set period where you must review and fine-tune your vision statement. I suggest you consider reviewing your whole vision statement once a year (see page 192). You may want to change parts of your vision more frequently. For example, if you use the vision map tool, your vision might change every six months to a year or so (see pages 178-186). You might have the same mission message for one year or for many years. Use your common sense and wisdom from your leader for knowing when to make changes.

Often, changes in career, the birth or adoption of a child, your health, where you live, or big changes in your finances, your involvement and responsibilities with your church family, among others, can be opportunities for fine-tuning your vision to reflect current reality.

Fine-tuning your vision can mean adapting or changing any or all of the components of your vision statement: your mission message, core values, or core beliefs.

You can make your fine-tuning process as simple or as involved as you want. I suggest you pray to God for wisdom to honestly evaluate where you are and where you sense may be the wisest direction for you to go in concerning your family vision. You may find the vision you tune in and live out may be a wise vision for your family for such a time as this and for years to come. However, you may find you are ready to fine-tune your vision in one to three years.

Heidi and I began fine-tuning our vision one night as an inspiration at the dinner table. We confronted our need for a new vision given our youngest were then almost two years old and joining in on our conversations easily enough. The light bulb went on for us: We knew the time had come to simplify our vision *big time*!

In the span of fifteen minutes, we hammered out our new mission message, beliefs, and values. We involved the kids as much as we could. In the weeks and months before we had talked about what our new vision would need to look like in being meaningful for our kids. We had prayed about our family visioning.

We tested our new vision statement with the kids for how meaningful the vision was for them. Our four-year-old was able to recite and meaningfully understanding our vision. Within a year, our boys were familiar with our vision and could recite it to others. By then they had nearly daily encounters with the vision in the give-and-take of our parenting them. Every week on Sunday evenings at our family gathering we would celebrate our vision and our *Strauch team* and its journey.

After dinner that night, I took time to prepare and write out our vision on a one-page sheet. Will this be the experience of most families fine-tuning their vision? Not likely. As our kids get older, our own fine-tuning will likely take more time and involve each member more in the process.

You can use or adapt the Yearly Review process described on page 192 for fine-tuning your vision. Depending on your family size, age-range, and logistics, you may want to consider doing the fine-tuning process away from home somewhere where you can be attentive and engaged with each other for an extended time. Whether you go to a park, a retreat center, a cottage by a lake, or create a visioning environment at home, be sure you do not go to a place where lots of interests compete for your time and attention. In other words, as a friend and colleague once said, make sure you are not distracted from your distractions by your distractions![107]

Be sure to use the visioning process described in Chapter 11, *The Visioning Process*. The Family *Vision Map* is an excellent tool for evaluating and discussing your current family vision and journey. Honestly evaluate how well your family lives out the vision it tunes in. Review chapter 10, *The Characteristics of a Vision,* to help you assess your vision. You will see where you stand in your progress on your journey. You will see and discuss your weak and strong areas and where you may want to adapt your journey.

Consider evaluating not just your vision statement but also what is and is not helping you to most effectively participate with God. Measure the effectiveness of your family gatherings against your vision statement. Assess which gathering tools are working best and which are not and why. If you see any problems in how your family does gatherings or uses tools, consider using the laser beam tool to brainstorm solutions.

You can use the *Self-Awareness Survey* on page 77, Figure 2, to reflect on your family's journey. You can use the survey in Appendix D, *Assessing Our Readiness*, to get your family's read on your current strengths and weaknesses.

The journey is not intended to be easy. Measure and assess yourselves not so much on your success as on your faithfulness. Most of Jesus' apprentices who traveled with him eventually were killed for being his followers and leaders with him for the world. Were they successful? By human standards, we'd say not. Yet by any measure we celebrate their faithfulness in telling and embodying the story of God for all.

Gratefully, the story of God is unfolding toward such time as when Jesus comes again. The story would have long since petered out, perhaps told as legend, were it not for folks like you and me, whose messy family and personal stories miraculously are being transformed into the unfolding story of the one whose story we live and tell. *Enjoy the journey!*

Family Journey Point: Chapter Eighteen

To Ponder: What do you imagine when you hear your family vision?

To Consider: Commit to being a follower of Jesus and a leader with Jesus.

To Remember: *"...You will tell everyone about me..."*
Acts 1:8b (CEV)

Appendix A

Bible Passages

For further reading and reflection:

- **Jacob's dream:** Genesis 28:10-22
- **Joseph reassures his brothers:** Genesis 50:15-21
- **Love the Lord your God:** Deuteronomy 6:4-9
- **The plans of the Lord:** Psalm 33
- **God's movement for the world:** Psalm 67; Acts 10; 1 Corinthians 9:19-23; John 17:20-21; Acts 1:4-8
- **Worship:** Psalm 95
- **God's love and faithfulness:** Psalm 100
- **Living out a vision:** Nehemiah 2:11-6:15
- **God is doing a new thing:** Isaiah 43:19
- **Managing what we are given:** Malachi 3:10
- **Prayer:** Matthew 7:7-8
- **Jesus' instructions:** Matthew 10:5-16; John 13:1-17, 35
- **Who Jesus is:** Matthew 16:13-19; 1 Peter 1:18-25; John 1:1-5
- **Who is the greatest?:** Matthew 18:1-6
- **Becoming a servant:** Matthew 20:25-28; 2 Timothy 3:16
- **The great commandment:** Matthew 22:34-40
- **The great commission:** Matthew 28:16-20
- **Sending out 12 apprentices:** Mark 6:7-13
- **Serving others:** Mark 10:44-45; Ephesians 4:11-13; Romans 12:6-21
- **Completing the work we're given to do:** John 17:4; Acts 2:42; Acts 13:36

Appendix B

More Examples of Mission Messages

We follow Jesus for the world

We hang out with Jesus and our neighbors

Being transformed, we help our neighbors experience transformation

We model Jesus to Mill Creek Homeowners Association

We embody Jesus for the benefit of the world

We are fueled by Jesus to transform our neighbors

We are transformed by Jesus to offer our friends transformation

With Jesus, we give friends hope

Released by Jesus, we proclaim release to the world

We help our neighbors experience Jesus' love

Freed by Jesus, we invite Johnson Creek to become free

With Jesus for the World

We follow Jesus in authentic teamwork for the world

Being the light of Jesus for the world

Appendix C

Brainstorming Your Mission Message

Let the ideas flow without hesitation or censure. Be kind to yourselves and do not judge what you write, think, or say. Just say and write what comes to mind. Be sure to review the brainstorming process guidelines on page 137 before you begin.

If a negative or doubting thought creeps in, simply acknowledge it and move on. Mentally set it aside or jot down your thought to address later on in your own journaling or conversation with a trusted friend. Later on, even the next day, you can look at what you write here in your brainstorm and see it with fresh eyes.

Proceed with passion and joy! You can grow in faith, become more like Jesus, partner with God in God's movement for the world, and nurture your own family as you journey.

Who we are:

____

____.

Who is Jesus to us:

____

____.

What we do:

____

____

____

____

____

____

____.

Who we can build transformative relationships with:

____

____

____

____

____

____

____.

The core benefit we can provide:

____

____

____

____

____.

Appendix D

Assessing Our Readiness to Live Out Our Vision

In assessing your readiness, rely upon God to challenge, support, and empower you. Ask questions that invite God to speak into your current snapshot of strengths and weaknesses. You can assess the readiness of your family to impact others' lives in the 21st century by asking questions such as these and exploring them together:

1. Are you committed to Jesus . . . or to your family?

2. Do you speak of faith as an experience with Jesus . . . or as a set of beliefs that you "pass down" to your children?

3. Do you believe that following Jesus involves reaching out for the benefit of the world ... or for the benefit of the family?

4. Do you worship with excited expectancy ... or with a sense of duty?

5. Do you guide and nurture friends, neighbors, associates, relatives, and perfect strangers to church, a small group, or outreach event . . . or do you wait for them to show up someday?

6. Do you value transforming lives ... or belonging to your family?

7. Does your family value radical commitment . . . or do you not expect much from your family members?

8. Have you discussed the kind of home and family life you want to create together . . . or have you put off that discussion?

9. Is God the leader of your family . . . or an adult member of the family?

10. Does your family encourage and accept those who don't follow Jesus . . . or does it feel threatened by them?

11. Does your family have a vision, core beliefs, and values . . . or a set of unspoken, unwritten, noncommittal principles?

12. Is every decision your family makes based on your vision, beliefs, and values . . . or just some or none?

13. Would your family rather do a mission trip . . . or Disneyland?

14. Does your family easily share about why you have a relationship with God . . . or would you rather they learn and discover without your sharing and on their own?

15. Does your family like asking or receiving difficult questions . . . or does it shy away from controversial or shady-area questions?

16. Does your family worship God all week, sometimes as a family at home . . . or one day a week with the congregation?

17. Does the Bible inform all that you do and are . . . or is the Bible an heirloom on the shelf?

18. Is your family accepting of all people . . . or some people?

19. Is your family accepting of yourselves . . . or critical of yourselves?

20. Does your family have lots of fun together . . . or is that asking too much?

21. Does your family see conflict as and opportunity for growing closer . . . or cringe at the onset of conflict?

22. Do you use money strategically for God . . . or for your family?

23. Do you value relationships . . . or religion?

24. Does your family have regular intentional family meetings . . . or does your family prefer to move with the ebb and flow of what happens?

25. Does your family pray for others regularly . . . or most only when there's an emergency need?

26. Does your family story live and express the unfolding story of God. . . or does your family story express some other story?

If you affirmed the first part of most questions, your family is poised to be part of what God is doing for the world in the 21st century. If you affirmed some of the first parts, and some of the second parts, you have just targeted your areas of change as you tune in your family vision and live it out. If you affirmed mostly the second parts of the questions, why don't you invest time and energy focusing on tuning in your family vision and living it out.

Appendix E

Survey of Strengths and Weaknesses

Which of the four essential aspects—faith, growth, mission, or nurture—is your family currently strong in and which are you weak in? Answer the following questions with 1 being an unqualified *Yes* and 10 being an unqualified *No*. Go with your first inclination.

The members of my family:

1\. . . . see themselves as always in an openly seeking mode.

1(yes) 2 3 4 5 6 7 8 9 10 (no)

2\. . . . have a deep sense of compassion and empathy for strangers.

1(yes) 2 3 4 5 6 7 8 9 10 (no)

3\. . . . make self-care a priority.

1(yes) 2 3 4 5 6 7 8 9 10 (no)

4\. . . . love asking hard questions and exploring difficult issues, even knowing that answers may be hard to come by.

1(yes) 2 3 4 5 6 7 8 9 10 (no)

5\. . . . seek to commit to projects that give their life away.

1(yes) 2 3 4 5 6 7 8 9 10 (no)

6. . . . enjoy reflecting on and then applying new ideas.

1(yes) 2 3 4 5 6 7 8 9 10 (no)

7. . . . like seeing their spiritual, mental, physical, and emotional selves as inseparable aspects of who they are.

1(yes) 2 3 4 5 6 7 8 9 10 (no)

8. . . . continue to grow in confidence and in understanding themselves better.

1(yes) 2 3 4 5 6 7 8 9 10 (no)

9. . . . see their life as inseparable from relationships with others on a journey.

1(yes) 2 3 4 5 6 7 8 9 10 (no)

10. . . . are confident in talking conversationally about their faith.

1(yes) 2 3 4 5 6 7 8 9 10 (no)

11. . . . aren't afraid to say, "You know, I'm not sure" nor are they afraid to say "One thing I am sure of and that is . . . ."

1(yes) 2 3 4 5 6 7 8 9 10 (no)

12. . . . are glad to be accountable for what they commit to doing.

1(yes) 2 3 4 5 6 7 8 9 10 (no)

13. . . . enjoy figuring things out and developing new skills.

1(yes) 2 3 4 5 6 7 8 9 10 (no)

14. . . . want to encourage and support healing and transformation in others.

1(yes) 2 3 4 5 6 7 8 9 10 (no)

15. . . . like to take action when they feel called or are a good fit for a project or task.

1(yes) 2 3 4 5 6 7 8 9 10 (no)

16. . . . love laughing, giggling, and playing with their family.

1(yes) 2 3 4 5 6 7 8 9 10 (no)

17. . . . like to wonder, "What if . . . ?" and then try out their idea.

1(yes) 2 3 4 5 6 7 8 9 10 (no)

18. . . . discover meaning through doing.

1(yes) 2 3 4 5 6 7 8 9 10 (no)

19. . . . experience a sense of humility, celebration, and joy.

1(yes) 2 3 4 5 6 7 8 9 10 (no)

20. . . . experience the holy in a way that transforms, deepens, and enriches them.

1(yes) 2 3 4 5 6 7 8 9 10 (no)

21. . . . would rather make decisions about their own project than about someone else's.

1(yes) 2 3 4 5 6 7 8 9 10 (no)

22. . . . seek opportunities to donate love daily.

1(yes) 2 3 4 5 6 7 8 9 10 (no)

23. . . . enjoy sharing with others what they are learning and discovering.

1(yes) 2 3 4 5 6 7 8 9 10 (no)

24. . . . are passionate about the people they serve and their needs.

1(yes) 2 3 4 5 6 7 8 9 10 (no)

Your survey results: Place the numbers you circled on their respective lines below. Add up the value of each column of numbers and place the total beneath on the ***Totals*** row:

Faith Aspect:	**Growth Aspect:**	**Mission Aspect:**	**Nurture Aspect:**
1. _____	4. _____	10. _____	3. _____
2. _____	6. _____	11. _____	5. _____
8. _____	7. _____	12. _____	14. _____
9. _____	13. _____	15. _____	16. _____
20. _____	17. _____	18. _____	19. _____
21. _____	24. _____	22. _____	23. _____
Totals:			
_____	_____	_____	_____

The lower your score for an aspect the stronger you are in that aspect.

Appendix F

Exercises to Explore

- **Group-Tell Family Story** (chapter 1): Have your family group-tell a story or event in the life of your family. Perhaps you went on a mission trip, a vacation trip, donated a gift to someone in need who didn't expect you to donate, or did a family project donating your time cleaning up an elementary school alongside the students' families in an impoverished area of the city. Agree on a story to tell. One person starts by introducing the story with "At the beginning...." The next person uses the connector, "and then..." to add more to the story. When one is aware that an aspect of the story is missing, the connecting words can be, "but before that...." Include people, their expectations, reactions, and ongoing impact.[108]

- **Beacon Game** (chapter 2): Have your children take turns being blindfolded and spun around several times. Their job is to find their way to another "beacon" family member standing in another part of the house or yard. The blindfolded person may ask the "beacon" person on two occasions to say, "Over here!" Other family members give guidance. Explore how hard this game is and how helpful the family and the "beacon" were. Explain that finding the beacon is a journey. Your family can team together in encouraging each other and God can be your leader guiding you on your journey. Also explain that your family vision, like the beacon, is an important way God can guide you.[109]

- **What do you dream of doing and being as a family?** (chapter 2)

   - In the next year?
   - In the next three years?
   - In the next ten years?

- Ask: "**Is there anyone whom you think we should help right now by praying for them with God?**" (you can pray for yourself or your family, if you want) (chapter 2)

- **Pretend Family game** (chapter 3): Pretend you are a different family for a moment. What is different about your pretend family? Explore together what anyone shares and envisions. Have the person to the left restate in different words what is shared. Make no judgments or negative statements about what any family members say. Let your imagination imagine! You may be surprised by what you learn about your family's perspective.

- **What would we like God to do for the individuals in our family right now?** (chapter 3)

- **What would we like God to do for our family right now?** (chapter 3)

- **The Hammer Illustration 1** (chapter 4): Get out a hammer, a piece of wood, and some nails. Pound in a nail or two. If I say hurtful things to someone else my words hurt. Pull the nail out. When I pull out this nail, what do you see? An empty, gaping hole. Your words are powerful. Like this nail pounded into the wood, they can create a deep hurt inside someone else.

- **The Hammer Illustration 2** (chapter 4): What is a hammer? A tool to pound nails—not your finger. So too your brain. It is a tool to help you, not to hurt you. Your words have power to help or hurt. Take charge of the words that swirl around in your head. If you trip and fall and disappoint yourself, don't say, "I'm such a klutz."

What does that accomplish? You become what you believe. Instead, focus on the positive and use the brain that God created for you to use. When your mind focuses on a negative message, see that message, cross it out in your mind's eye and throw that message away. Then move on to create a new positive message, "I am able (smart, beautiful, loving, wise, funny, caring, kind); I can do this; I have what I need to do this" or "I am learning from everything I do."[111]

- **Rhythm Group** (chapter 5): Sit in a circle. One person starts to make a sound and continues making it at a regular rhythm (e.g., snap, clap, wind sound). The next player adds a new sound and rhythm to the mix. Go all the way around the circle adding new sounds, rhythms and discovering your very own performance band. If you have a small group the players change their sound each time it is their turn. Reflect on how your family is connected together, where each person's role and behavior impacts the whole of your family. **Variation (especially fun with smaller children):** Let everyone pick out a spoon or other make-shift instrument to make the sounds.

- **Personal History** (chapter 5): (1) Invite each family member to write down on a slip of paper one thing that the others do not know about you. Everyone puts their slip of paper in a hat and a facilitator passes the hat around; each person selects one slip of paper (not their own). Each person takes a turn to read their slip of paper and guess who wrote that note about themselves. (2) Each family member explains what was the most important or difficult challenge they faced as a child (if the member is a child, help them to explore what they found difficult earlier in the day).

- **Self-Awareness Survey:** Invite each member to complete the survey on page 74. If you are comfortable, share what you wrote.

- **Explore the Assessing Your Strengths and Weaknesses questions:** Individually and separately review and jot notes in response to each question in Appendix D. Then explore together your responses and observations about your family in response to the questions.

- **Explore the Survey of Strengths and Weaknesses:** Individually and separately complete the survey in Appendix E. Explore together your answers and results, sharing them as each is comfortable doing so.

- **Make a pizza or other favorite dish with the children** (chapter 6). Explain that all the ingredients are each part of the whole pizza. In the same way, learning about and following Jesus, growing more like him, serving other people like Jesus does, and caring for and loving each other and ourselves are each important parts of our journey with God.

- **Explore the Breath Prayer** (chapter 7): Using the method described on page 91. With your children, practice using the phrase "I am a child of God" (Psalm 46:10). Describe and explore together your experiences with this form of prayer. Use other phrases, as you feel led to.

- **Memorize this verse** (Luke 5:15-16 CEV) **but with this change** (chapter 7): "But (your name) would often go to some place where s/he could be alone and pray." Explore with each other how memorizing and reciting this verse affects you and what times are best for you to spend time with God within you.

- **Memorize this verse** (2 Corinthians 3:18 MSG) **but with this change** (chapter 8): "I am bathed with light as God enters my life." Explore with each other how memorizing and reciting this verse affects you. Help younger children experience this verse. Read it for them and substitute their names in for them. Can you accept and believe this passage for your life?

- **Molding Clay** (chapter 8): Using clay or play dough, create a shape with your clay or dough for the person sitting on your right. Create something you know they want, or something that they will smile about or appreciate. Your imagination is your only limitation. Describe your shape and why you created it for the person. Explore how you are currently being shaped by God.

- **Magazine/School Yearbook/Newspaper Pictures** (chapter 9): Have either individuals or pairs (an adult with each small child) pick a magazine (school yearbook or other) picture that piques or speaks to them. Then ask the following questions and provide paper and pencils or crayons for the prayers. What do you know about this picture? Where do you see God? Write or draw a prayer for the picture. Share the picture and the prayers with the others. Explore how through prayer you can be a special help for others.

- **Telephone** (chapter 9): Line up, front to back. Have the person in back of the line whisper a sentence in the ear of the person in front of you but while everyone talks aloud. That person repeats what s/he heard into the next person's ear and so on down the line. Listen for what comes out at the end. Repeat this process with the person in back whispering clearly but while everyone else is silent. Notice that the clearer the message starts out the more likely it will get through the line. Explore how having a family vision will help you be a team.

- **Clear Message** (chapter 9): Take five minutes and go into separate rooms. Then say something sweet that you know will make your partner smile, perhaps something about how much you love your partner. Then call each other on your respective cell phones and tell them the same message. Come back together. Explore how having a clear compelling family vision is like having a direct line to each other and to God that will help you be a powerful team with a clear message.

- **Making Rain** (chapter 13): Sit in a circle or semi-circle. Choose a leader for this exercise. The leader prompts the others by making eye contact to do whatever sound s/he is doing. At some point, the leader changes the sound by example and prompts with eye contact for the others to do likewise. Use your imagination: Sound one could be rubbing hands together; sound two could be snapping fingers, alternating hands; sound three could be patting thighs, alternating hands; and, sound four could be stomping feet or hitting hard surface with palms. Build up the storm and then reverse the motions to end with a quiet, light rain. Explore how being in sync together can be beautiful and meaningful and requires the actions and participation of every teammate.

- **Ear to Elbow** (chapter 13): Begin by milling around the room randomly. Have a facilitator call out two body parts. Find a partner and connect the two body parts as quickly as possible. Everyone remains connected while the facilitator calls out two more body parts. Seek to connect body parts as called out to do until you can no longer pretzel yourself into new connections! Explore how being connected with each other is fun and how family gatherings are a way to be connected. Examples of potential body part connections–knee to back, head to stomach, elbow to nose.

- **What you like about your loved one** (chapter 13): Sit silently together; decide who will start. If it suits your style, light a candle, or place a Bible in the middle of the table, anything that helps you be aware of the presence of God. The first person completes the statement, "What I am gifted in and passionate about is…." After that person has spoken, observe a short time of silence. This person now invites their loved one to share. Using the same process, move on to a second statement, "What I like about you is…" (See pages 167-168 for more details).

- **Write down observations** (chapter 14): Observe your family over a period of an agreed time (One week? Two weeks? One month?) and write down your perceptions vis-a-vis the six modes and your family's behavior. Share your written observations and discuss.

- **Share with the others** about which tool in chapter 15 most attracted your attention or jumped out at you and why.

- **Play-acting** (chapter 15): Read aloud a children's Bible version of a story about Jesus (e.g., feeding-of-the-5,000, healing a blind man, calling disciples to follow, etc.). Creatively play-act the story using props (towels make good robes). As much as possible, allow children to take the lead, play important roles, and creatively bring the story to life. Let your imagination have free sway.

- **Learning** (chapter 15): Invite each member to find a short Bible passage or verse, person, story, or tidbit to share with the others. Each person gets familiar with and researches their chosen topic. Come together and learn from the presenter and their topic in a gathering (see pages 185-186 for more details). Explore how learning from, and being encouraged by, each other–no matter our age, ability, or maturity–can be exciting and enriching.

- **Accepting Others** (chapter 16): Agree as a family that for one month you will emphasize two beliefs: "God perfectly loves everyone" and "we love everyone like God does." Apply these two beliefs to everything you do and are as a family for this one month. Observe what happens and how you apply these beliefs as a family. Share with each other your observations and stories. Decide whether or not to continue practicing this kind of love.

- **Serve together** (chapter 17): Brainstorm on a service project for a neighbor, friend, or group. Use the brainstorming process described on pages 132-135. As much as possible, let the younger members take the lead and creatively generate ideas. Pray for wisdom to make wise decisions. Once you have agreed on a project, plan for it, schedule it, and have fun with it!

- **Story-telling** (chapter 17): Briefly share, in a simple way, the story of the first time God's love for you in Jesus became real to you. Or, alternatively, share what you have heard or learned about God from others (friends, pastors, movies, television, books, the Bible).

- **Dreaming** (chapter 18): Imagine it's two years from today. You are sitting with a long-lost friend underneath and in the shade of a large oak tree on a hillside overlooking your house. You feel a gentle warm breeze in your face. You are describing to your friend the remarkable journey you and your family have journeyed the last two years. What do you say? Describe, or draw a picture of, your family as you imagine them interacting with each other during this time. Share and explore what you have written or drawn. How does what you wrote or drew strike you?

Appendix G

Why Use So Many Translations?

The Bible is infinitely rich with wisdom and truth for our lives today. Reading the Bible is like holding a gem which refracts light differently with every twist and turn, revealing new combinations of light, color and space. In the same way, using different translations of the Bible can allow us to experience Bible passages differently than perhaps we might have before, bringing new wisdom, truth, and insight into our lives. Even excellent translations have some limitations. Using a variety of translations, we may be helped in being encountered by God in what God has to say for our lives.

Notes

Chapter 1. Seeing Your Family's Journey as a Story

1. Matthew 23; Luke 11: 37-54.

2. Mark Mittelberg, ***Building a Contagious Church: Revolutionizing the Way We View and Do Evangelism*** (Grand Rapids: Zondervan Publishing House, 2000), p. 37.

3. Proverbs 29:18-19.

Chapter 2. It All Begins With God

4. Janet Butler [pseud.], telephone conversation with author, 7 February 2008.

5. Matthew 5:48.

6. Passages used to support a belief in God's constant, specific direction for Christians include: Ephesians 5:15-17; Colossians 1:9; Romans 12:1-2; Proverbs 3:5-6; 1 Corinthians 14:40; Colossians 3:15.

7. James 3:13; Proverbs 9:12, 21:11; Ecclesiastes 7:19, 8:1.

8. Romans 8:29; Colossians 1:15; Ephesians 4:22-24, 4:22; 2 Corinthians 3:18; Philippians 2:13; Romans 12:2; Ephesians 4:13.

9. Luke 17:20-21.

10. Sy Safransky, "Notebook," *The Sun* (February 2008).

Chapter 3. Choosing To Be Transformed

11. Story submitted by Claire Toaspern.

12. Genesis 15:1; Deuteronomy 33:29; 2 Samuel 22:3, 22:31; Psalm 3:4, 5:13, 7:10, 18:2, 30, 28:7, 33:20, 59:11, Psalm 115, 119:114, 140:7, 144:2; Proverbs 30:5; Ephesians 6:16; 1 Peter 1:5; Isaiah 59:17; Ephesians 6:17; 1 Thessalonians 5:8.

13. Ephesians 6:16-17; 1 Peter 1:5.

14. Ephesians 6:17.

15. Luke 17:20-21; Matthew 28:20; Acts 1:8.

16. Psalm 27:3.

17. Revelation 3:20.

Chapter 4. Your Family

18. Mark 5:19.

19. William Faulkner, Act 1, Scene III of Requiem for a Nun.

20. Romans 7:19.

21. While we have Jeremiah 31:34, God forgives "(Israel's) wickedness and will remember their sins no more," we don't have Biblical instruction that we should forgive and forget, necessarily. This is especially an important understanding for those who've been victimized by abuse, violence, or dangerous behavior.

22. Telling the Truth: Preaching About Sexual and Domestic Violence, Chapter 4, Preaching Forgiveness? Marie M. Fortune, pp 49-57, explores forgiveness in the context of domestic violence. (United Church Press, Cleveland, OH, 1998).

23. Romans 12:1-2.

Chapter 5. The Family System Story

24. Adapted from ***Generation to Generation***, "Coaching One Parent With Emphasis on the Nuclear Family," Edwin Friedman, (The Guilford Press, 1985), p. 114-115.

25. I was first introduced to the Polarity Theory and Management by The Alban Institute. ***Discerning Your Congregation's Future: A Strategic and Spiritual Approach***, Roy M. Oswald & Robert E. Friedrich, Jr., (Alban Institute, 1996), pp 32-48.

26. Matthew 10:1-16, 7:24-27; Luke 10:1-16.

27. Matthew 10:30.

Chapter 6. A Thriving Family

28. Bill and Connie Anderson [pseud.], telephone conversation with author, 25 February 2008.

29. I am indebted to Patrick Lencioni and his use of the triangle to depict the skills of a team in his book, ***Overcoming the Five Dysfunctions of a Team: A Field Guide for Leaders, Managers, and Facilitators,*** (Jossey-Bass, 2005), p. 6.

30. Matthew 26:42.

31. Matthew 5:23-24.

32. Galatians 6:2-5.

33. Adapted from ***Growing Spiritual Redwoods***, William M. Easum and Thomas G. Bandy, (Abingdon Press, Nashville, 1997), p. 15-152.

Chapter 7. Tuning In To God

34. ***Seven Minutes With God***, Richard Foster, NavPress (Colorado Springs, Colorado).

35. Titus 3:5-7; 1 Corinthians 2:10; Romans 8:14; Acts 1:8.

36. 1 John 4:19.

37. Romans 5:10 (NLT); John 15:15.

38. Ecclesiastes 4:12.

39. 1 John 5:13.

40. Romans 12:2.

41. Video shown at Mosaic Church, Portland, OR, during Moriss Dirks' message on 6 July 2008.

42. John 14:6-7, 14:9-11.

43. John 1:1-4, 10:9, 14:6.

44. 2 Timothy 3:16-17.

45. John 4:26.

46. Gary Thomas, ***Sacred Pathways: Discover Your Soul's Path to God***, (Zondervan Publishing House, Grand Rapids, MI, 1996); book explores nine spiritual temperaments.

47. Matthew 22:37; John 4:24.

48. Genesis 1:26, 2:7, 22; Psalm 82:6; John 10:34; Jeremiah 1:5.

49. John 15:4.

50. Jack Hayford, ***Why I Don't Set Goals***. Article first posted 7/12/2007 on *Building Church Leaders*, an e-newsletter produced by Christianity Today.

51. Matthew 4:19, 21; 9:9; Mark 1:17; 20; 2:14; Luke 5:10, 27; John 1:39, 43.

52. Matthew 20:32; Mark 10:36, 51; Luke 18:41; John 1:38.

53. I stumbled upon this practice in my work moderating administrative boards; I am indebted to friend and colleague, La Vae Robertson, who encouraged me in the use of this practice. I am also indebted to the authors, Dennis Linn, Sheila Fabricant Linn, Matthew Linn, of ***Sleeping With Bread: Holding What Gives You Life***, (Paulist Press, 1995).

54. I am indebted to Andrew Dreitcer and his resource, *Lectio Divina with a Group*, Program in Christian Spirituality, San Francisco Theological Seminary, June 1996. I am also indebted to Cynthia Bourgeault and her audio program, ***Encountering the Wisdom Jesus: Quickening the Kingdom of Heaven Within,***

a six-part audio workshop from soundstrue.com.

55. James 1:22.

Chapter 8. The Characteristics of a Follower

56. Janet Butler [pseud.], telephone conversation with author, 7 February 2008.

57. Matthew 28:20; 2 Corinthians 4:14; Acts 13:2, 7:55, 2:33; 1 John 2:1.

58. Colossians 3:12; Ecclesiastes 3:4; Matthew 9:36, 14:14, 15:32, 20:34, James 5:11; 1 Peter 3:8.

Chapter 9. The Power of a Vision

59. James Johnson [pseud.], emails with author, 15 May 2009.

60. 2 Corinthians 12:9, 12:10, 13:4.

61. Acts 20:24; Matthew 28:18-20; John 14:12.

62. Romans 8:29; Colossians 1:15, 27; 2 Corinthians 4:4; Hebrews 1:3; Ephesians 4:22-24; Matthew 5:1- 12; Galatians 5:22-23; 1 Corinthians 13; 2 Corinthians 3:18b; Philippians 2:13; Ephesians 4:13.

63. John 3:16; 1 John 3:1, 3:16, 4:7, 16-19; Ephesians 2:4, 3:18; Matthew 5:48; Luke 15:11-32.

64. Super Nanny show, "The Drake Family," January 2, 2008, ABC.

65. W.H. Murray, ***The Scottish Himalayan Expedition***, (1951).

66. Matthew 28:20.

Chapter 10. The Characteristics of a Vision

67. Genesis 1:26.

68. Matthew 28:19; 1 Corinthians 10:31-33; 2 Peter 3:9.

69. 1 Peter 1:16; Leviticus 11:44-45, 19:2, 20:7; Deuteronomy 6:5, 10:12, 11:13; Joshua 22:5; Matthew 22:37; Mark 12:30; Luke 10:27.

70. Galatians 5:22-24.

71. John 15:8; Ephesians 2:10: Colossians 1:10.

72. Mark 10:27; Luke 1:37, 18:27; Matthew 17:20.

Chapter 11. The Visioning Process

73. Luke 10:1-17; Matthew 28:18-20; 10:1-42; Mark 6:7-13; 3:13-19; Luke 9:1.

74. I am indebted to Ron Kincaid and his book, ***Praying for Guidance: How to Discover God's Will***, (InterVarsity Press, Downers Grove IL, 1996), to Garry Friesen and his book with J. Robin Maxson, ***Decision Making and The Will of God***, (Multnomah Press, Portland OR, 1980), a course Friesen references as taught by Norman Shawchuck at Trinity Evangelical Divinity School, and to Victoria G. Curtiss and her resource ***Guidelines for Communal Discernment*** (Presbyterian Distribution Service, Louisville KY, PDS#24358-08-007).

75. 1 John 4:7-11, 16, 18; 1 John 3:16; John 3:16; Matthew 7:11; Luke 11:13, 12:24, 28; Ephesians 3:18; Deuteronomy 7:9; Zephaniah 3:17; Romans 8:39.

76. I am indebted to Ronnie Noize and her ***Killer Elevator Speech*** e-book (www.ronnienoize.com) for introducing to me and coaching me in what she calls "the elevator speech." I have adapted her elevator speech concept.

77. p.89 of BusinessWeek magazine, May 17, 2004, *The Power of Design* by Bruce Nussbaum; courtesy of Ideo, a design firm .

Chapter 12. Living Out the Vision

78. Acts 15:12-18; John 3:16; Matthew 7:11.

Chapter 13. Family Gatherings

79. Genesis 37:50.

Chapter 14. Six Modes of Family Gatherings

80. I am indebted to Craig R. Hickman, ***Mind of a Manager, Soul of a Leader,*** for his exploration of the tension between management and leadership. John Wiley & Sons, Inc., 1992.

Chapter 15. Twelve Tools for Family Gatherings

81. Briana and Caleb Turner [pseud.].

82. I adapted what Patrick Lencioni calls the *lightning round* in his book, ***Death by Meeting: A Leadership Fable***, (Jossey-Bass, 2004), p. 238.

83. Eric H.F. Law, *The Wolf Shall Dwell with the Lamb: A Spirituality for Leadership in a Multicultuiral Community*, (Chalice Press, 1993). Introduction adapted from Eric H.F. Law's ministry, The Kaleidoscope Institute.

84. I am indebted to friend and colleague, La Vae Robertson, who first introduced to me this practice. I am also indebted to the authors, Dennis Linn, Sheila Fabricant Linn, Matthew Linn, of ***Sleeping With Bread: Holding What Gives You Life***, (Paulist Press, 1995).

85. Charles M. Olsen, ***Transforming Church Boards - into communities of spiritual leaders***, Alban Institute 1995. p. 52-80.

86. Matthew 18:19-20; Nelsen, Jane, Ed.D., ***Positive Discipline***, New York: Ballentine, 2006, pp. 208-209.

87. Nelsen, Jane, Ed.D., ***Positive Discipline***, New York: Ballentine, 2006, pp. 208-209.

88. Ibid.

89. I have adapted Patrick Lencioni's *Family Scoreboard* concept outlined in his book, ***The 3 Big Questions of a Frantic Family***

as a way of making visual and shorter a much more involved in-depth strategic planning process.

90. David Robinson, ***Family Cloisters: Benedictine Wisdom for the Home,*** The Crossroad Publishing Co., New York, 2000.

Chapter 16. One-On-One Relationships

91. Paul Tillich's phrase, "accept your acceptance".

92. Matthew 5:48.

93. Romans 12:4-5; 1 Corinthians 10:16-17; 12:12-27; Ephesians 1:22-23; 2:15-17; 3:6; 4:4-13, 16; 5:30; Philippians 3:21; Colossians 1:18-20, 24; 2:19; 3:15; Hebrews 13:3.

Chapter 17. Family Leadership

94. Matthew 26:39.

95. John 15:12-15.

96. Matthew 28:18-20.

97. 2 Corinthians 5:21.

98. John 1:1-4, 14, 29.

99. John 11:25; John 14:6; John 10:18; Mark 10:34; Colossians 2:14; Ephesians 1:19-20; Philippians 4:13; John 17:3; (see also: Matthew 16:21, 17:23, 20:19; Mark 9:31; Luke 9:22, 13:32, 18:33, 24:7, 24:21, 24:46; Acts 10:40; 1 Corinthians 15:4);

100. John 14:26; 1 Corinthians 2:13; Ephesians 3:5; Acts 1:8, 2:4; Romans 8:11, 15:16; 1 Corinthians 2:10, 12:3; 1 John 5:4-5; Luke 4:1; John 7:38, 14:16.

101. Luke 10:1-17, abbreviated and adapted from ***The Message*** by Eugene Peterson.

102. Matthew 28:18-20 (NIV).

103. I am indebted to Mark Mittelberg, Lee Strobel, Bill Hybels, and Wendy Seidman in adapting guidelines set out in ***Becoming a Contagious Christian: Communicating Your Faith in a Style that Fits You***, pp 124-149, Zondervan Publishing House, Grand Rapids, Michigan.1995.

104. John 14:6.

105. I heard this anecdote from Rick Warren's message, "*What Difference Does Easter Make?*," published by Preaching Today, tape number 223.

106. I am indebted to Jane Nelson, Ed.D. and her book ***Positive Discipline***, pages 208-209. New York, Ballantine. 2006.

107. I am indebted to many for this process, including Stephen Covey and his audiotape, ***The Seven Habits of Highly Effective People.***

Chapter 18. Fine-Tuning Your Vision

108. Mark Yaconelli, Summer Conference Retreat, Bend, Oregon, 2008.

Appendices

109. Charles M. Olsen, ***Transforming Church Boards - into communities of spiritual leaders,*** Alban Institute 1995. p. 52-80.

110. Mimi Doe with Marsha Walch, PH.D., ***10 Principles for Spiritual Parenting: Nurturing Your Child's Soul,*** (HarperPerennial, 1998).

111. Ibid.

Personal Notes:

Breinigsville, PA USA
25 September 2009
224747BV00002B/6/P